BEYOND THE BLUE GLASS

BEYOND THE BLUE GLASS

Catholic Essays on Faith and Culture

Volume I

Aidan Nichols, O. P.

THE SAINT AUSTIN PRESS
296, Brockley Road
London, SE4 2RA

Telephone: +44 (0)20 8692 6009
Facsimile: +44 (0)20 8469 3609

Electronic mail: books@saintaustin.org
http://www.saintaustin.org

ISBN 1 901157 16 4

Typeset and printed by Newton Printing Ltd, London, UK.   www.newtonprinting.com

...Visible, invisible

powers, presences, in and beyond the blue
glass, radiantly-occluded Sion, pour
festal light at the feet of the new poor,
scavengers upon grace...

Geoffrey Hill, *Hymns to our Lady of Chartres*

ACKNOWLEDGEMENTS

The author and publishers are grateful for the following permissions to reprint:

The Thomist, for an earlier version of Chapter 2, "Thomism and the *Nouvelle Théologie*", in Vol. 64 (2000), pp. 1-19.

T. and T. Clark, for an earlier version of Chapter 4, "Littlemore from Lucerne: Cardinal Newman seen by Cardinal Balthasar", in I. Ker (ed.), *Newman and Conversion* (Edinburgh 1997), pp. 100-116.

The Heythrop Journal, for an earlier version of Chapter 5, "Balthasar's Aims in his *Theological Aesthetics*", in Vol. XL. (1999), pp. 409-423.

Antiphon: A Journal for Liturgical Renewal, for an earlier version of Chapter 8, "Odo Casel Revisited", in Vol. 3. 1 (1998), pp. 12-20, and for an earlier version of Chapter 9, "A Tale of Two Documents: *Sacrosanctum Concilium* and *Mediator Dei*", in Vol. 5. 1 (2000), pp. 23-31.

Communio: International Catholic Review, for an earlier version of Chapter 10, "Hymns Ancient and Postmodern: Liturgy as Consummate Philosophy", in Vol. XXVI. 2 (1999), pp. 429-455.

They are especially indebted to Professor Geoffrey Hill for allowing a phrase from one of his poems to serve as the title of the collection, and for permission to reprint lines from *Hymns to our Lady of Chartres*, from *Collected Poems* (Penguin 1985), and *New and Collected Poems 1952-1992* (Houghton Mifflin Co., Boston and New York 1994).

CONTENTS

PREFACE

The reception of an essay collection, *Scribe of the Kingdom*, has emboldened me to offer another set of essays to the public. Once again, the themes are theology, and philosophy, the Liturgy and the arts – though I have added here some thoughts on ecumenism, both of the historic variety which happens between Christians and of the "new" or "wider" kind, which concerns itself with the followers of other religions or that vaguer religiosity that is contemporary neo-paganism. And, as before, the touchstone is "epiphany"[1]: the illuminating and transforming impact of a plenary Catholicism on a world which already participates by the creative action of God, in the divine fullness of being and goodness, truth and beauty. The motto I suggested in the opening piece of the first collection ("intelligent conservatism") suffered perhaps from inappropriately political connotations.[2] That did not prevent a distinguished critic, the Anglican bishop-theologian Rowan Williams construing its meaning aright, as the acknowledgement that the Church's assured teaching has an epistemological priority over the deliverances of other sources of knowledge, and the nuanced awareness that the tradition of the Church is articulated in several media or styles, in art as in philosophy, so that theological renewal or *ressourcement* has to be a *cultural* enterprise in the widest sense.[3] I believe those are very Dominican convictions, and in these new volumes I engage rather more than previously with the classical inheritance of the Order that is Thomism – and, of course, Thomas.

Blackfriars,
Cambridge,
Memorial day of St Boniface, 2000.

---

[1] See my *Epiphany: A Theological Introduction to Catholicism* (Collegeville, Minn. 1997).

[2] For my attempt at a theology of civil society, see *Christendom Awake: The Re-energizing of the Church in Culture* (Edinburgh 1999), pp. 71-90.

[3] R. Williams, reviewing *Scribe of the Kingdom: Essays on Theology and Culture*, 2 vols. (London 1994) in *New Blackfriars* 76. 892 (1995), p. 203.

PART ONE

THEOLOGY

I

ST THOMAS IN HIS TIME

St Thomas was born in 1225 into a pro-imperial Italian aristocratic family, the de Aquinos, who had land and a castle at Roccasecca, half way between Rome and Naples, just to the east of that great thoroughfare, the Via Latina. His parents – Lombard on his father's side, Neapolitan on his mother's – sent him to the boarding school run by the monks of Monte Cassino and arranged for him to become an oblate there, planning so to make use of their local influence as to have him, in due course, elected to the abbatial dignity. For Cassino was, to the feudal nobility of the region, a great prize. When he was fifteen, however, and could have made solemn profession (the oblateship was understood in this period in a way which makes it comparable to simple profession in the modern Latin church), the abbot of Monte Cassino advised his parents to send him, rather, to the emperor Frederick II's *studium generale* at Naples – probably because skirmishes between emperor and pope were making Cassino too hot for comfort.[1] He would have lived, no doubt, in the Neapolitan study house owned by the Cassinese monks, the dedication of which, a significant pointer to the half-Greek character of southern Italy in the Middle Ages, was to St Demetrios of Thessalonica.[2]

Naples was a cosmopolitan place, as were generally southern Italy and Sicily under the influence of a ruler who sat lightly to his own religion (and anyone else's). There Thomas was introduced by one Michael the Irishman to the latest ideas in the shape of the natural philosophy of Aristotle.

---

[1] T. Leccisotti, "Il dottore angelico a Montecassino", *Rivista di filosofia neoscolastica* 32 (1940), pp. 511-547.

[2] J.- P. Torrell, O. P., *Initiation à saint Thomas d'Aquin, Sa personne et son oeuvre* (Fribourg 1993), pp. 7-8.

Arab astronomy and Greek medicine would also have been capital in this University milieu. Catching a whiff of pagan naturalism at Naples was important: in Paris at the same period the study of Aristotle was officially forbidden.

At the age of nineteen Thomas joined the newly instituted Order of Friars Preachers – a priory had been founded at Naples in 1231 by Jordan of Saxony, St Dominic's successor. He did so in the teeth of opposition from his family, who resorted to such low tricks as abduction and (attempted) seduction: abducting Thomas while he was on his way, in the entourage of the Master of the Order, John the Teuton, to the 1244 General Chapter in Bologna, and attempting to seduce him by introducing a prostitute from the camp following of their military retinue into his room at Roccasecca, during his "house arrest". The claim that the reason for their opposition was social embarrassment, much as if a son of the Duke of Buccleuch had absconded from Eton to become a hippy in Islington, though widely made by socially radical Thomists in the 1960s, looks less plausible when we learn that the friar who gave him the habit, his namesake Thomas de Lentini, shortly after became bishop of Bethlehem, papal legate and patriarch of Jerusalem. Benedictine influence would in any case linger in the form of Thomas's habitual citation of Gregory the Great (nearly two thousand five hundred times), and especially of the latter's *Dialogues*, on the life and miracles of St Benedict, which Thomas drew on heavily in his theological defence of the Religious life. Thomas's last known writing is a letter of 1274 to abbot Bernard Ayglier of Monte Cassino where, as his most recent biographer, Père Jean-Pierre Torrell, writes, he "refound spontaneously his language as a young monk and presented himself as 'a son always ready for prompt obedience'". [3]

In all probability, St Thomas passed over to the Dominicans chiefly because he saw there greater opportunities for the study and communication of the fruits of contemplation to others for which he had already developed the aptitude at Cassino – though we cannot rule out as a possible secondary factor in his

---

[3] Ibid., p. 21.

renunciation of life in that well-endowed monastery a desire for evangelical simplicity. Père Chenu called his departure from Cassino "the exact replica of the gesture of Francis of Assisi",[4] inasmuch as St Francis repudiated his father's wealth, St Thomas the great riches of his abbey. In his treatise in support of the friars, Thomas will call Religious poverty an outstanding lesson of the Cross of Christ.[5]

Whatever the blend of factors in his motivation, it was typical of Thomas that he used his enforced leisure at Roccasecca to read the Bible right through and to begin his study of contemporary theology. Blind to blandishments, then, Thomas persisted, powerfully aided no doubt by the excommunication and deposition of Frederick in 1245. Henceforth Aquino hostility to a papally mandated Order lost its *raison d'être*. Making doubly sure of their candidate, however, the Order despatched him for the completion of his noviciate, and subsequent study, to Paris, the pre-eminent University city of the age. We have from this student period, in Thomas's handwriting, the commentary of St Albert the Great on Dionysius the Areopagite's *On the Celestial Hierarchy*, produced in the characteristic *peciae* or separate fascicules which were the hallmark of Parisian manuscript production. Given the unspeakable awfulness of St Thomas's handwriting, if, as some scholars suggest, Albert was deliberately employing him for this purpose as a secretary, the great German philosopher-theologian must have been singularly impractical – or kind-hearted. From Paris, the young Thomas set out to accompany his master when in 1248 Albertus Magnus returned to Germany with the mission of founding a new general study house of the Order at Cologne. It was at Cologne that Thomas would have heard Albert lecture on *The Divine Names* of Denys, the paramount source for the Christian-Platonist element in Albertine thought, as later in his own, and also on the *Ethics* of Aristotle, all ten books of which had just been translated for the first time by bishop Robert Grosseteste of Lincoln. Almost certainly it was at Cologne that Thomas was

---

[4] M.-D. Chenu, O. P., *St Thomas d'Aquin et la théologie* (Paris 1959), p. 11.
[5] *Contra Retrahentes*, 15. I owe these points to Père Torrell's magisterial study.

ordained priest. And above all it was at Cologne that he began, modestly enough, his professional teaching career as a "biblical bachelor", with literal commentaries on Jeremiah and the Book of Lamentations, as well as on Isaiah, though the *Super Isaiam* also included spiritual exegesis in the form of marginal notes.

In 1252, the Dominican Master-General John of Wildeshausen, anxious to strengthen the rôle of the friars at Paris, was prevailed upon to return Thomas, whose outstanding gifts had already been noted, to the Ile-de-France. Accordingly, at an age below the normal, and after relatively abbreviated preparation, he graduated that year as a bachelor in theology, a sort of junior lecturer whose task it was to comment on the *Liber Sententiarum* of Peter Lombard, a systematically thematic presentation of texts from the Fathers on the articles of the Creed – *sententiae patrum*, "the views of the Fathers" – and the theological manual in most widespread use ever since the Fourth Lateran Council had strongly recommended it in 1215. Thomas's commentary on the Sentences, the *Scriptum super Sententiis*, is far from being merely footnotes to Lombard, however, for Aquinas introduces a new principle of organisation – of theological intelligibility – all his own. He considers all things inasmuch as they come forth from God, the Alpha or absolute Beginning, in dependence on the procession from the Father of the Word, and inasmuch too as they return to God, the Omega or absolute End, by the grace which depends on the procession from Father and Son of the Holy Spirit.[6] Thomas provides us here with a first sketch of the plan of his future *Summa Theologiae*, the "Summa of Theology", with which his name will always be connected. Indeed, it now seems that even ten years later Thomas was still working on improvements of this five thousand page work, something known from the discovery of an alternative, more incisively argued version, at Lincoln College, Oxford, in the 1970s. Meanwhile he

---

[6] F. Marinelli, *Personalismo trinitario nella storia della salvezza: Rapporti tra la ss.ma Trinità e le opere ad extra nello "Scriptum super Sententiis" di San Tommaso* (Rome 1969), and, more widely, G. Marengo, *Trinità e creazione: Indagine sulla teologia di Tommaso d'Aquino* (Rome 1990).

also found time to help out his brethren, who were floundering, evidently, in the swamps of metaphysics, by writing two small treatises, *On Being and Essence*, and *On the Principles of Nature*, where we have a first glimpse of his debt to the Arab philosophers, and to their Jewish contemporary, Maimonides. Here we see in action that "intellectual charity" which formed so distinctive an aspect of his sanctity.[7]

By the time Thomas had finished even the first version of his commentary on Lombard, he was no longer a simple bachelor. In 1256, at the exceptionally early age of 31, Thomas became one of the twelve masters of the Sorbonne – a sort of mediaeval equivalent to the holder of a chair in a modern Faculty of Divinity. His rôle was to raise, discuss and resolve theological problems on the basis of, above all, his biblical knowledge: hence the title *magister in sacra pagina*, "master of the sacred page". He was fortunate in this, since his appointment coincided with the climax of a campaign against the friars mounted by the secular masters in the course of which the French king, Louis IX, had to send archers to protect the Dominicans against the secular clergy and populace. Thomas was assisted by the bull of Pope Alexander IV, *Quasi lignum vitae*, which bade the chancellor of the University quell the uproar of the secular masters against the friars and give them their rights. In thirteenth century terms, his task was a threefold one: *legere, disputare, predicare* – to comment on Scripture, to dispute, to preach. We see him at work in this period in these three distinct ways when, firstly (*legere*), we read his commentary on Matthew, the full text of which was discovered only this century in a library in Basle (Switzerland); when, secondly (*disputare*), we study his "disputed questions" *de Veritate*, "on truth", or, thirdly, (*predicare*) we dip into his University sermons – preserved, alas, so differently from Newman's, only in note form. (The Sunday and feast-day sermons, passed down in the *opera omnia* of Thomas in times past, are now recognised as

---

[7] J.-P. Torrell, O. P., *Initiation à saint Thomas d'Aquin*, op. cit., p. 72.

spurious.[8]) And of course, on top of all this, Thomas had to do his bit in setting out a theological case for the presence of the friars among the professors. Here his thesis was that no work of spiritual mercy – and preaching and teaching were for him certainly that – is unfitted to be the distinctive purpose of a Religious order.

Parisian chairs changed hands rapidly, and, strange as it may seem, at some point in 1259 Thomas found himself at rather a loose end. The next year or so of his life is shrouded in obscurity; it is probable that he returned to Italy, where the historian soon finds him. From a whole variety of indices, ingeniously assembled by scholars (they range from the character of the parchment and ink Thomas used, to developments in both his documentation and his doctrine as well as back references in other treatises), we can infer that it was in this shadowy period that Thomas started composing the *Summa contra Gentiles*, the first of his two masterpieces. The claim was made in the sixteenth century that Thomas wrote this work as a "missionary handbook" for Catholic representatives in the world of Islam, but attention to its contents suggests a wider aim: negatively, convicting of error those who brought arguments against the faith from a great diversity of standpoints, from out-and-out pagans to Christian heretics, and, more positively, of showing the beautiful intelligibility of the suprarational wisdom of divine revelation, where the truths of philosophy fructify in their definitive, God-provided context. Since Thomas died before he could finish the successor to the *Summa contra Gentiles*, the *Summa Theologiae*, it is to these earlier syntheses of theology that we must look for his account of eschatology, the last or ultimate things.

In the autumn of 1261 St Thomas was named conventual lector of the priory of Orvieto, a little Umbrian city with an outsize cathedral, perched on an isolated and almost perpendicular outcrop of rock, originally an Etruscan fortress and later a refuge in times of distress for the mediaeval popes. One supposes that Thomas's duties were not especially exigent, and it is from the

---

[8] L. J. Bataillon [O. P.] "Les sermons attribués à saint Thomas: Questions d'authenticité", *Miscellanea mediaevalia* 19 (1988), pp. 325-341.

Orvieto period that we have the widest variety of his writings – most commonly produced in response to requests from correspondents near and far, whether eminent or virtual nobodies. Thus Thomas's analysis of the views of the Greek Fathers on the issues increasingly separating the Greek and Latin churches was made at the request of the pope (it was unfortunate that so few of the excerpts in the anthology Thomas was sent were authentic) while the treatise *On the Reasons for the Faith* was put together for an anonymous "cantor of Antioch" – a minor cleric in the crusader State in Syria. Other short books were despatched to an Umbrian archdeacon and a Sicilian archbishop.[9] Here too, in all likelihood, Thomas wrote the most Christian-Platonist of all his works, the *Commentary on the Divine Names*, from the pen of that mysterious Greek-speaking Syrian Christian of the sixth century who went by the name of Dionysius the Areopagite, a companion of Paul in the Acts of the Apostles; the *Commentary on the Book of Job* (generally regarded as the best crafted and most penetrating of his biblical works), the *Catena Aurea* or "golden chain", an exposition of the four gospels from texts taken from the Fathers (which the still Anglican Newman valued so much that he had a team of Tractarian scholars translate it)[10], and, not least, St Thomas's only known poetry, the liturgical office for the newly introduced feast day of Corpus Christi (promulgated as an intrinsic part of the Roman liturgy by Urban IV in 1264). Thomas's expansion of his knowledge of the Fathers and Councils of the Church in his Orvieto period doubtless owes much to the fact that the archives of the papal curia were currently based in what was now his home town.

"Now" – but not for much longer. In September 1265, the Roman Province of the Order, to which Thomas belonged, asked

---

[9] The *Expositio super primam et secundam Decretalem* (the Fourth Lateran Council's confession of faith and its reprobation of the theology of history of Joachim of Flora); and the *De articulis fidei et Ecclesiae sacramentis* respectively.

[10] See my "Introduction" to the republished edition, *Catena Aurea: Commentary on the four Gospels collected out of the works of the Fathers by Saint Thomas Aquinas* (London 2000), I., pp. v-xxi.

him to go south to Rome itself, and set up a house of studies in the City – almost certainly at Santa Sabina, the residence of the Master. The late Father Leonard Boyle, Prefect of the Vatican Library, believed this was a unique experiment, what he termed a *studium personale*, essentially a one-man study centre where Thomas was free to develop courses as he thought fit.[11] The fact that it did not survive his departure from Rome is therefore entirely unsurprising. The title of Boyle's study, which argues this case, "The Setting of the *Summa Theologiae* of Saint Thomas", makes plain the claim to glory of Thomas's stay at Rome: it was then that the most important of all his works was conceived. Just when and where the different parts of the *Summa* were actually published is a matter of scholarly debate, but perhaps the dominant view would ascribe the *Prima Pars* to Rome, the *Secunda Pars* to Paris (on Thomas's return there in 1268 or 1269), and the *Tertia Pars* to Naples, when in his ending he returned to where his University studies had begun.

The *Summa Theologiae* opens by asking what theology is, and its answer is that theology is orderly reflection on the content of revelation, biblically attested as this is, and summed up in the articles of the Creed. This orderly reflection is carried out in the light of God's own knowledge of himself and his saving plan – which light, as communicated to ourselves, we call "faith". It is, then, in the broadest possible terms, an integration of faith and reason, and while Thomas allows that charity may give the unlettered person a kind of intuition or instinctive judgment in matters of faith, normally it requires study and hard work. The rest of the *Summa* falls into three parts which follow broadly what has been termed an *exitus-reditus* – literally, "coming out, going back" – scheme. The fount or source of creatures is God whose existence is, for Thomas, known by reason but the mystery of whose being, in its concrete character, requires revelation for its description. After describing this fontal being, which is totally complete self-communicating goodness expressing itself through

---

[11] L. Boyle O.P., *The Setting of the "Summa Theologiae" of Saint Thomas* (Toronto 1982).

the interplay of three subsistent relationships (Father to Son, Son to Father, Father and Son to Holy Spirit), Thomas considers the issue from God of the created world: first, that of pure minds, the Angels; then, that of the natural order as a whole, and finally the place of man, who is embodied mind or perhaps better (in Thomist anthropology) intellectualised body. Creatures come forth from God, structured in the way that natural philosophy indicates but dependent on God for their existence and in the case of rational creatures ordered to him by their tendency to seek a goal beyond themselves.

Thus the first "part" of the Summa, the *Prima Pars*. The second part begins by an account of human happiness which is, for St Thomas, the purpose of morality, just as it was for Aristotle. Thanks to the doctrines of creation and redemption, however, the content of such happiness must be re-described so as to include – indeed, centre on – the vision of God. This is our aim and destiny, "return" to God in beatification. Thomas then uses a combination of Aristotelian ethics and the ascetic and moral writings of such Church Fathers as John Cassian and Gregory the Great to give an account of the basic emotional drives of human nature and how these, like mind and will, are distorted by sin. So ends the first half of the second part of the *Summa*, entitled less cumbersomely in Latin the *Prima Secundae*.

Next comes the first explicit treatment of the difference Christ makes: the gift of a new interior principle of acting, Christ's Holy Spirit. Thomas explicitly puts the question, What is the Gospel in itself? Is it, for instance, morals, or cultus, or teaching to be believed? He answers that primarily it is none of these things but the power of a new love which unites us with God and with each other. The teaching element, the written Gospels, dispose us to receive this Holy Spirit; the sacraments actually mediate this life to us, and it proceeds spontaneously to express itself in Christian living. The Spirit of Christ supernaturalises our natural drives not just through modulating the moral virtues but also and more specifically in two particular ways – the "theological virtues", new God-directed dispositions, and the "Gifts of the Holy Spirit".

First, then, that Spirit elicits faith, hope and charity, which make us tend to the God of the saving revelation as he is in himself, giving us real contact with him. And secondly, he bestows on us those gifts or endowments proper to the messianic child in the Book of Isaiah, applied by Church tradition at large to the messianic people of the New Covenant and associated by the Latin church with, especially, Confirmation. For Thomas the Gifts essentially concern making the Christian life easy: they enable us to love God and our neighbour in thought, word and deed with happy facility.

The remainder of the *Secunda Secundae* is what we might call a phenomenology – a reflective description – of the Christian life, a life informed by charity and articulating itself in both practical goodness and contemplation. This enables Thomas to sum up in the final question of this "second half of the second part" his earlier broadsides against those secular clergy of the time who had attacked the friars as interlopers. The best way to be a Christian is to unite contemplation and practical goodness; the highest form of practical goodness is to pass on understanding of the Christian faith, since this alone is helpful not only for time but also for eternity; so the best way to follow the Gospel is *contemplata aliis tradere*, to "give to others the fruits of contemplation" – in other words, to become a Dominican!

The third and concluding part of the *Summa* shows what actually made (and makes) possible this return of rational creatures to God. Having spoken of our origin and our goal, Thomas must now make clear the path that connects them, and this he identifies as Christ, the *iter ad Deum*, or pathway to God. The incarnation, life, death and resurrection of the Word, bring together the origin and the goal, and we encounter them in their salvifically connecting capacity in the sacraments which, for Aquinas, are efficacious symbols – signs that actually bring about what it is they signify. As he will write on the *iter ad Deum* in *Compendium Theologiae*:

> The totality of the divine work finds its completion in that man, the last created creature, returns to his source by a kind

of circle, when by the work of the Incarnation he finds himself united to the very source of [all] things.[12]

Convenient as it may be at this juncture to offer an overview of the shape of the *Summa Theologiae*, I am running ahead of the story. Something more needs saying about the other works of Thomas's Roman period, and indeed of his second, very fruitful, engagement as professor in Paris – not least because for contemporaries, whatever may be the case for us today, the *Summa Theologiae* did not prove (to judge by the diffusion of manuscripts) the sort of *succès de réclame* that might have been expected. Or, to put the matter more fairly, it would be known in the Middle Ages more by vulgarisers and abbreviators than for itself. From the Roman period we have, for instance, the *De Potentia*, "*On the Power* [*of God*]", a series of disputed questions crucial to Thomas's metaphysics of the creation – for him at once totally dependent on God and yet (or rather, *and therefore*) totally free to be itself; the little jewel called the "Compendium of Theology", where we find a very simple and moving précis by Thomas of what it is we believe in and hope for; more answers to questioners, and the first of his commentaries on the texts of Aristotle, a treatment of the *De anima* – perhaps suggested by the fact that much of his recent work, like the *Prima Pars* of the *Summa*, had obliged him to consider more closely the nature of the human creature, as a unity of body and soul.

Why Thomas was made, or chose, to return to Paris, we can only conjecture. The scholars suggest that the reason lay in the deteriorating intellectual situation (for an orthodox Christian, for a Dominican, for a sympathiser of Thomas's kind of thought) in that academic capital of thirteenth century Latin Christendom. What was at stake was threefold. Firstly, there was well-founded anxiety over doctrinal orthodoxy, for a school of Latin – and thus, in principle, Christian – supporters of the Muslim philosopher Averroes had arisen, who maintained (through, it would seem, a tendentious misreading of their master's teaching) that human

---

[12] *Compendium Theologiae* 201.

beings share one universal mind, and thus can expect no personal immortality. Secondly, there was the question of the retention of influence by the Order, for the crying havoc of the secular masters had started up again. And thirdly, under threat were also the rights of citizenship within the Church of what would later be called "Thomism" – for conservative theologians hostile to the use of that rather too earth-bound philosopher Aristotle were bent once more on a formal condemnation of the use of his writings in Catholic thought. All of which helps explain why the personal presence of Thomas was deemed desirable if not indispensable – as also the fact that so much of this second professoriate at Paris was taken up with expounding and where necessary salvaging from "Averroist" interpretation the works of Aristotle. It was as though Thomas foresaw, and attempted vainly to forestall, the bitter disputes precipitated at Paris by his death.

For although the Platonism of Saint Thomas is quite as important as his Aristotelianism, it was the Aristotelianism which was controversial. Aristotle had asked, fundamentally, two questions. What is reality like, and what are the rules of argument which get us from one conclusion about it to another? The first kind of question is answered in his *Physics*, *Metaphysics*, and *Ethics*; the second in his logical writings, the *Organon*, a name we can paraphrase as, "the philosopher's tools of trade". The latter had been percolating through, in dribs and drabs, for some time, but a logical rule is empty unless you have some content for it to deal with, and it was the philosophical and ethical writings that caused the stir. In them, the different kinds of things in the world around us, including man, are analyzed in terms of general principles of being and action which all beings in different ways exemplify; happiness is said to be the goal of specifically human life; it is reached by the exercise of virtues which are ways of being at harmony with myself and my human environment. There is little in Aristotle about the divine, for the philosopher lacked the concepts both of creation and of the personal nature of God, even if he saw a place for an unmoved Mover to keep the whole cosmic process of coming-to-be and passing-out-of being in operation.

26

Thomas's achievement was to integrate such naturalism into the traditional Christian vision of life which the earlier monastic theologians entertained. In the early middle ages theology had been by and large the spiritual theology practised in the monasteries. While issues of logic were beginning to exercise monastic minds (one thinks of St Anselm), and such ruminations on the fundamental grammar of theological discourse were even more at home in cathedral schools, the aim was predominantly (not least in Anselm) the expression of the prayerful orientation of man to God. Preferred theological themes were closely relevant to spiritual living: religious self-knowledge, one's status as creature and sinner; the grace of Christ and how it heals from sin and raises up to share the life of God; the goal of earthly pilgrimage in the beatific vision, sitting down with the Trinity at the banquet of heaven in the celestial city. Monastic theology, so well described in Dom Jean Leclerq's *The Love of Learning and the Desire for God*, included, as that title tells us, ardour for erudition.[13] The same monastic milieux transmitted, after all, much of the pagan classical inheritance as well as the Church Fathers. It was Thomas's conviction, evidently, that this programme could be taken much further. The naturalism of the pagans at their best – the thinking, both theoretical and practical, of the "good pagans" – could be textured into the fabric of Christian theology, without losing – and here is the point that Thomas's more rationalist disciples in later centuries were in danger of forgetting – the spiritual and eschatological (in a word, the *heavenly*) – orientation of theology itself.

It is from his second Parisian period that we have, at least very probably, Thomas's treatise "On the Eternity of the World", which accepted, against the English Franciscan John Peckham, the philosophical case that in principle the world might always have existed, while maintaining against neo-paganising naturalists that we know from revelation that in fact this is not the case. Around the same time, Thomas produced his book "On the Singleness of

---

[13] J. Leclerq, O.S.B., *The Love of Learning and the Desire for God: A Study of Monastic Culture* (Et New York 1961, 1974).

the Substantial Form", where he argued (not especially originally, for a generation earlier, among the first of the high mediaeval Scholastics, this view had been fairly general) that the same soul, form of the body, carries out at different levels all the functions, from mere physiological growth to the highest reaches of contemplation, of which the human person is capable. One of the fears here was that, to deny, as Thomas did, a distinct *bodily* form might mean in Christology that we cannot say of the body which hung upon the Cross that it rose self-identically on Easter Day (since, evidently, its intellectual form, the rational soul, had been separated from it in the meanwhile). For Thomas, however, the identity of the body of the Passion and that of the Resurrection is guaranteed by the fact that the divine Word is its enduring subject. The *De unitate intellectus*, against the "monopsychism" of the Latin Averroists, already mentioned, belongs here too.

Thomas now took further two of the three classic genres of his first Parisian period which correspond so neatly to the three chief duties of a theological master in his time. He brought out his great commentary on John (he may well have seen this as the rightful successor to his work on Matthew: the first gospel of the Canon could stand for the second and third, since all three Synoptic evangelists were primarily theologians of the Saviour's humanity, the fourth evangelist of his divinity). And he resolved a great range of "disputed questions", many belonging to the "question-box", or "ask what you will", variety known as *quodlibets* which most of the masters assiduously avoided, since in such perilous games of intellectual self-exposure reputations could all too easily be lost.

If we do not have examples of his preaching to be assigned with security to these years, then the lacuna is filled by a medley of minor compositions whose subject matter ranges from the angels, and the metaphysics of the Platonists, through scientific cosmology and topics that raise the issue of Providence like astrology and making choice by lot, to questions of social ethics such as how to treat the Jews. And above all, this is the great period of Thomas's work on clarifying and interpreting the corpus of Aristotle. His exposition of two of Aristotle's logical writings, the *Peri Hermeneias* and the *Posteriora Analytica*, are, naturally enough, among the most technical of his works, yet the way his wider philosophy enhances the coherence of Aristotle's text has been admired.

The *Sententia libri Ethicorum*, Thomas's re-writing of Aristotle's *Nicomachean Ethics*, is, however, more ambitious than that: the Gospel re-makes morals; it leaves logic largely as it was. The commentaries on the *Physics* and *Metaphysics* of Aristotle testify to Thomas's perennial interest in the structure of nature and its relation to its Prime Mover – but also to his determination to "read" the Greek philosopher via his own creationist metaphysic of being, which was far from Aristotle's mind. However, he never completed studies of some other minor treatises of Aristotle on the physical world, nor for that matter his commentary on the latter's *Politics*. In all these enterprises, we should note how Thomas is not primarily concerned with the historical reconstruction of texts from the fourth century before Christ: to think so would be on our part both an anachronism and a serious under-estimate of the *apostolic* aim of all Thomas's writing. Rather was his intention in seeking the original author's mind so to seek the truth, a truth clearer in the light of revelation than to Aristotle himself.

When Thomas came to the end of his second period of Parisian teaching in 1272, less than four years of life were left to him, and the sheer expenditure of energy on so massive a literary output (contemporaries commented on the frenetic way he worked wrote or dictated, in sharp contrast to the later idealisation of the serene, eternity-absorbed master, or even the early memories of a bovine and therefore presumably placid "dumb ox") must have taken its toll – even if he did use secretaries, amounting perhaps in his later years to what Torrell calls "a veritable workshop of literary production."[14] But there was no rest for the wicked, or in this case, the righteous, as indeed the more sharp-witted contributors to the Wisdom Books of the Old Testament

---

[14] J.-P. Torrell, O. P., *Initiation à saint Thomas d'Aquin*, op. cit., p. 365.

had long ago noted. Assigned to Naples, he was given once again the task of creating a study house of the Order, this time no personal affair, however, but a *studium generale* in a city which would remain, until the late eighteenth century, among Europe's greatest capitals. As befitted one whose earthly span, though he knew it not, was closing, the subject matter he now taught was, in its period, non-controversial and apt for contemplation: the Psalter, the Pauline letters and the mysteries of the life of Christ which were to form the lion's share of the last part of the *Summa Theologiae*. It is thought-provoking that Thomas's presentation of the life of the Saviour, while from one viewpoint absolutely straightforward – a re-statement of the narrative structure of the Gospels themselves – is, to judge by the way he entitles its chief parts, a sort of *reprise* of the *Summa* so far: he begins with the *egressus*, or coming forth of Christ from God into this world; moves onto the *progressus*, or development of his public ministry, before attending to his *exitus*, or redemptive leave-taking of the world to return to God, and subsequent *exaltatio* or raising to God's right hand as the mediator of human glorification.

That *Tertia Pars* was, as already mentioned, never completed. Thomas fell into a trance while celebrating Mass in the chapel dedicated to Saint Nicholas in the priory at Naples, some time around St Nicholas's day (6 December) 1273 – later remarking that, in comparison with what he then saw, all his writings were as straw. He never set pen to parchment again. Thomas died on a journey between Naples and Rome, on the Appian Way, while obeying the injunction of the pope, Gregory X, to take part in the Second Council of Lyons, one of the abortive reunion councils between West and East, which was to open on 1 May 1274. The probable cause of death was a blood-clot, caused by hitting his head against a low-lying branch while on donkey-back. The monks of the nearby Cistercian abbey of Fossanova nursed him in his last days, and hours, and were rewarded for their pains by an improvised commentary on the Canticle of Canticles, the great love song of Yahweh and Israel, Christ and the Church.

Thomas died among the sons of Benedict just as he had lived with them as a child; and this was fitting because his theology, no matter how speculative its flights, had never had an ultimate goal different from that of Benedict or Bernard in the city of God.

II

THOMISM AND THE NOUVELLE THÉOLOGIE

The purpose of this essay is to consider a particular incident in the theological history of this century, but one with a significance extending beyond its own time and place. And this is the intellectual clash of arms between the chief representatives of what would shortly be called *la nouvelle théologie*[1] – Jean Daniélou, Henri de Lubac and others, and the classical French Dominican Thomism of the *Revue Thomiste*, in the years 1946 to 1948. The Dominican intervention was an important moment in the chain of events that led to the promulgation of Pius XII's encyclical *Humani Generis*, in 1950, on false trends in modern teaching, and to the eclipse – temporary in nature as it would prove – of the reputations of de Lubac and the others which followed in that encyclical's wake. The wider significance of the episode is that it raises the question of the relation between, on the one hand, the Thomist tradition, and on the other that neo-patristic theology, consciously open to certain aspects of modernity while retaining a primary allegiance to the Christian sources in Bible and Fathers, which can be regarded as the chief inspiration of the Second Vatican Council, and the predominant theological influence on the pontificate of John Paul II. One has only to ponder the fact that both leaders of the *nouvelle théologie* mentioned above were made cardinals, either by Paul VI or the present pope, whereas their main Dominican critic, Marie-Michel Labourdette, entered the most total obscurity until the present youthfully zealous editor of the *Revue Thomiste* devoted an entire issue to him, under the

---

[1] For general accounts, see: A. Darlapp, "Nouvelle Théologie", *Lexikon für Theologie und Kirche* VII (Freiburg 1963), p. 1060; T. Deman, "Französische Bemühungen um eine Erneuerung der Theologie", *Theologische Revue* 46 (1950), pp. 61-92; A. Nichols, O. P., *Catholic Thought since the Enlightenment: A Survey* (Pretoria and Leominster 1998), pp. 134-138.

title *Un maître en théologie*, in 1992.[2] Owing to a combination of perfectionism and the wounds sustained in this struggle which the French Church historian Etienne Fouilloux does not hesitate to call

> the only theological debate of any importance at least in France, between the condemnation of Modernism and the Second Vatican Council, [3]

Labourdette would largely restrict himself for the future to writing notices of books for the *Revue Thomiste* though, admittedly, these were both numerous and judicious. In the course of the 1970s he was removed from teaching at the Dominican study-house in Toulouse, owing to what his biographer, Henri Donneaud calls discreetly "les malheurs des temps".[4] His principal work, the *Cours de théologie morale* – a commentary, but of a speculative and at times original kind on the *Secunda Pars* of Thomas's *Summa Theologiae* – has enjoyed a posthumous career of much sought after duplicated or photo-copied existence for many years.

The story opens with the publication in 1946 of an essay entitled *La théologie et ses sources* by Père Labourdette, professor in the Dominican studium of the Province of Toulouse (at that time situated at Saint-Maximin in Provence) and editor of the *Revue Thomiste*, where the offending article appeared. It took the form of a studied criticism of two projects just launched by the French Jesuits: *Sources Chrétiennes*, under the general editorship of Jean Daniélou and Henri de Lubac, and the series *Théologie*, which was under the direction of the Jesuit faculty of Lyons-Fourvières with, as its secretary, Henri Bouillard, an historical theologian specialising in the theology of grace. In point of fact, *Théologie*, which had by the time of Labourdette's writing produced eight volumes, had begun life in 1944, while *Sources Chrétiennes*, which

---

[2] *Un Maître en théologie: Le Père Marie-Michel Labourdette, O.P.* = *Revue Thomiste* XCII. 1 (1992). Cited below as MT.

[3] E. Fouilloux, "Dialogue théologique? (1946-1948)", in S.-T. Bonino, O.P. (ed.), *Saint Thomas au XXe Siècle: Actes du colloque Centenaire de la "Revue Thomiste". Toulouse, 25- 28 mars 1993* (Paris 1994), p. 153. Cited below as DT.

[4] H. Donneaud, O.P., "Une Vie au service de la théologie", in MT.

had clocked up a total of ten, had been going since as early as 1942. But at that time of course Europe was involved in a global conflagration, in which Labourdette himself had been a military chaplain and, subsequently, prisoner of war. Indeed he had only just recovered the editorship of the *Revue Thomiste* entrusted to him for the first time in 1936 at the strikingly early age of 28. Though singling out for praise one of the *Théologie* works, Labourdette expressed grave reservations about the two series as a whole and called for a pacific but far-reaching debate on the nature and task of Catholic theology in their light.

Naturally enough, Labourdette had no objection to people making more readily available the writings of the Greek Fathers as such – for this was the aim of the early volumes of *Sources Chrétiennes*. No more did he think it reprehensible that, as with *Sources Chrétiennes'* sister series, *Théologie*, Catholic scholars should investigate the history of Christian doctrine. But he nonetheless divined in both series what would now be called a "hidden agenda", and one unacceptable to a disciple of St Thomas. For such a one, Scholastic theology alone represents, as Labourdette put it, Christian thought in its truly "scientific" state. While admitting that many of the products of Neo-Thomism left a good deal to be desired, he expressed himself as totally unwilling to jettison the proverbial baby with the bath-water. The two collections were, he thought, animated by a spirit of disapprobation of, and even contempt for, the Scholastic and especially the Thomist achievement and worse still by a depreciation of intelligence in its search for abiding truth. The two series were tainted by a relativistic attitude – relativist in two senses, as he went on to explain. Not only were their authors affected by historical relativism, treating truth as truth for this or that historical period – Henri Bouillard, notoriously, had written at the conclusion of his study of St Thomas's theology of grace that a theology that fails to be contemporary to that extent is false[5]; they were also influenced by an experiential relativism, where a

---

[5] H. Bouillard, *Conversion et grâce chez S. Thomas d'Aquin* (Paris 1944), pp. 219-220.

subjectivism of "inner experience" or "spirituality" could undermine the objective value of the truths of faith. The slope on which they had positioned themselves, the better no doubt to dialogue with Existentialists and historical materialists, was an impossibly slippery one which could only end in the evacuation of the idea of speculative truth, of time-transcending truth and even, ultimately, of truth itself.[6]

Who was thus placed in the line of fire? Those specifically mentioned, all Jesuits, are Bouillard, Hans Urs von Balthasar, Gaston Fessard, de Lubac, Pierre Teilhard de Chardin, but above all, Daniélou, mentioned unfavourably six times, five of them in connection with his 1946 essay "Les orientations présentes de la pensée religieuse" which had just appeared in the Jesuit journal *Études*.[7] It seems likely that Labourdette regarded Daniélou's short study as the key to the hidden agenda of the two series, so it is evidently incumbent on us to gain an overview of its content.

Daniélou's survey of current Catholic theology and philosophy falls into three parts. The first describes the movement of *ressourcement* with its return for inspiration to early Christianity through the biblical revival, the patristic revival and the liturgical revival. But, so Daniélou goes on to maintain in the second, central, panel of his triptych, such forms of return to the sources cannot by themselves guarantee the renewal of Catholic thought which the post-War world demands. For philosophies of suspicion have arisen – he has in mind both Existentialism and Marxism – which are appealing either to the historical process or to the personal struggle for identity. Catholic thinkers, Daniélou goes on, must not hesitate to follow the representatives of these alien philosophers onto their own home ground, the better to respond to them, as figures like Teilhard de Chardin and Gabriel Marcel were, he mentions, currently doing, if not always with

---

[6] M.-M. Labourdette, O.P., "La Théologie et ses sources", *Revue Thomiste* XLVI. 2 (1946), pp. 353-371.
[7] J. Daniélou, S.J., "Les orientations présentes de la Pensée religieuse", *Études* 249 (1946), pp. 5-21.

complete success. And Daniélou concluded this part of his article by affirming that some kind of phenomenological method should henceforth become the basis for, at any rate, all theology that set out to describe "religious realities in their concrete form".[8] Finally, Daniélou went on to say how stirrings in the lay apostolate were challenging philosophers and theologians in these areas: "activists" (these were still halcyon years for "Catholic Action") and the faithful at large were seeking not just a spirituality but also a theology that would answer their specific needs. Though never mentioning St Thomas by name, Daniélou gives the distinct impression that Scholastic theology will not be playing much rôle in all of this. It is, he intimates, an obsolete stage in the development of Christian thought. It is now time to move on – and perhaps more than time. He speaks of Scholasticism as an increasingly rationalist and desiccated theology, detached in an abusive sense from spirituality, and above all peculiarly unsuited by its own genius to what a contemporary sensibility requires.

> It is very plain that Scholastic theology is strange to these categories [of historicity and subjectivity] which are at the heart of contemporary reflection. Its world is the immobile world of Greek thought where its mission of incarnating the Christian message was lived out. This conception retains a permanent and ever valid truth to this extent at any rate: that it consists in affirming that man's decision for freedom and his transformation of the conditions of life are not an absolute beginning where he acts as his own creator, but rather humanity's response to a divine call itself expressed in the world of essences. And yet... [Scholastic theology] gives no place to history. And moreover, locating reality as it does more in essences than in subjects it ignores the dramatic world of persons, of universal concretes transcending all essence and only distinguished by their existence – that is, no longer distinct from one another by intelligibility and intellection but by value and love – or hate.[9]

---

[8] Ibid., p. 17.

[9] Ibid., p. 14. We should probably see in Daniélou's references to "love" and "hate" the influence of Max Scheler's "phenomenology of love and hatred", which Scheler presents as a basis for the apprehension of value (but not of the values themselves).

Neo-Thomism, like the Pontifical Biblical Commission, Daniélou goes on, was a railing (*un garde-fou*) to keep Modernism at a safe distance. But a railing cannot count as a reply, and though Modernism had been a false answer it had set a real question. Daniélou's manifesto, then, even if its primary purpose was to trumpet the glories of *ressourcement* and the need to engage with contemporary thought, had as a subsidiary purpose the marginalisation of Scholasticism in this new context. Some of its points were easily countered – Leonine Thomism for instance could hardly have been a defensive reaction to the Modernism not yet conceived when it was born. But enough darts had struck home to anger and even distress.

What gave these darts especial force was, in the first place, Daniélou's reputation and secondly, the fact that, though de Lubac is never mentioned by name in "Les orientations présentes de la Pensée religieuse", it was *his* already impressive body of work that Daniélou was implicitly putting forward as the model for French theology in the future. Daniélou, author of a Sorbonne doctoral thesis on Gregory of Nyssa, professor of Christian origins at the Institut Catholique, editor of *Études*, creator of the review *Dieu vivant*, and coming from an unusually secular background for a French cleric, or Religious, of the period (his family were staunch republicans and he had studied at non-Catholic University faculties prior to entering the Society), was someone who both intimidated and alarmed more conventional or at least typical Catholics. De Lubac, his Jesuit mentor, was well-placed to serve as the very model of a modern Catholic apologist – what with his 1938 study *Catholicisme*, where he set out to show how effective the Fathers could be in a self-consciously state-of-the-art presentation of the faith, and his 1944 *Le drame de l'Humanisme athée*, with its sympathetic enterings into the minds of Dostoevsky or Nietzsche the better to answer their queries. But even Yves Congar – no opponent of historical theology he – had been moved to write privately to de Lubac on the publication of his *Corpus*

Mysticum,[10] a study of the relation between the Eucharist and the Church in patristic and pre-Scholastic mediaeval thought, reproving him for an attack on Scholasticism which, however, de Lubac simply denied it had ever been the least part of his intention to make.

And yet these two figures alone would surely not have sufficed to cast the Thomist and Dominican camp in France into a slough of despond, or at any rate a sense of aggrieved victimhood. And in fact there was more. The War and the German occupation, during which period both Marxism and Existentialism had made major strides, had significantly altered the cultural climate, rupturing links with the world of the 1920s and 1930s where the Thomism of Jacques Maritain, Etienne Gilson and the Dominicans themselves had been widely discussed by believer and unbeliever alike. The Fribourg Thomist Charles Journet wrote in 1945 to Maritain, "In this disintegration of the world, if you try to stay faithful to St Thomas, they think you're mad".[11] A new outlook was entering the Church which Maritain, for his part, did not hesitate to call "anti-intellectualist". Greater precision can be given that word on the basis of a second letter from Journet who complained of a tendency to

> put between brackets the conceptual formulation of maybe even the revelation but certainly the theology and philosophy we have received from the Middle Ages, ... [which tendency] tries to rejoin the Greek Fathers to the extent that their doctrine is tacit, not to mention preferring a formulation that plays on a conceptual keyboard borrowed from Hegel and Existentialism.[12]

This Journet associated both with de Lubac and what he called his "entourage", as well as with the Dominican Augustin Maydieu, a figure heavily involved in the Resistance and subsequently editor of *La Vie Intellectuelle*, the organ of

---

[10] Exchange of letters 27 February – 1 March 1947, in Archives de la province jésuite en France, described in DT, p. 165.

[11] Letter of 9 August 1945 in Archives des Cercles Jacques et Raïssa Maritain at Kolbsheim, cited in DT, p. 158.

[12] Letter of 27 December 1945 in the same archive, cited in ibid.

philosophical and theological *haute-vulgarisation* of a Paris Province less concerned with Thomist consistency than was its neighbour of Toulouse. In an unpublished article of the same period, Maritain summed up Journet's anxieties in a memorable phrase as theologians "reinventing the Fathers of the Church to the music of Hegel".[13] It is worth noting that Maritain was Labourdette's great intellectual inspiration – on becoming editor of the *Revue Thomiste*, he had at once written to Maritain, not just seeking his help and collaboration but frankly placing the journal under the patronage of Maritain's ethical, intellectual and spiritual ideas. As he wrote in a letter of November 1936:

> On arriving at the *Revue Thomiste*, I could not fail to consider somewhat as a programme the defence and illustration of the ideas developed in *Science et Sagesse* and *Les Degrés du Savoir*, as also the rehabilitation of the true notion of what theology is, so impoverished as this has been since Melchior Cano [the Spanish Dominican moved by his reading of Cicero to propose that theological treatises should be constructed as surveys of theological monuments, *loci theologici*]. This is why I count so much on you and your friends ...[14]

"your friends" – of whom Journet was, in Labourdette's estimation, second only to Maritain himself. Finally, the anonymous underground circulation of works which would never have obtained a nihil obstat, mostly ascribed to Teilhard de Chardin and his fellow-Jesuit Yves de Montcheuil (shot by the Germans before the War ended), helped to convince Labourdette that, in Fouilloux's words, "a concerted enterprise of destabilisation of the Scholastic method was at work in France",[15]

---

[13] H. Donneaud, *Une vie au service de la théologie*, art. cit., MT, p. 25. It was true that *Fessard's* philosophical method was precisely to compare Hegel's *Phenomenology of Spirit* to Blondel's *L'Action*. See N. H. Gias, *Le Verbe dans l'histoire:* *La philosophie de la historicité du P. Gaston Fessard* (Paris 1974). On this figure, see M. Sales, "Bio-bibliographie du P. Gaston Fessard", in G. Fessard, *Eglise de France, prends garde de perdre ta foi* (Paris 1979), p. 286.

[14] Letter of 13 Novembre 1936, Fonds *Revue Thomiste*, cited in MT, p. 26.

[15] DT, p. 159.

of which the two series, *Sources Chrétiennes* and *Théologie*, were only the tip of the iceberg.

De Lubac, in keeping with his much cooler tone, compared with Daniélou, indicated to Fessard that he had no intention of replying to the forthcoming attack in the May/August 1946 issue of the *Revue Thomiste*. But events decided otherwise. On 17 September 1946, Pius XII delivered an address to the General Congregation of the Society, at which de Lubac was present. He heard the pope refer in a context apparently uncomplimentary to the "new theology". Two days later, offprints of Labourdette's essay, joined with a critical review of *Corpus Mysticum* by Labourdette's confrère Père Marie-Joseph Nicolas in the same fascicule, arrived on de Lubac's desk. What was happening? In part, if we are to look at the events in terms of general history, the political divisions of French Catholicism were beginning to express themselves by proxy. De Lubac, deeply committed to the Resistance, was supported by the newly empurpled pro-de Gaulle cardinal Saliège of Toulouse against attacks on his theological approach sent semi-clandestinely to Rome by the erstwhile supporters of Marshal Pétain and the régime of Vichy, or even, for that matter by members of the nationalist-monarchist Action Française now thirsting for some form of revenge after the years their movement had spent in the ecclesial wilderness. (Proscribed by Pius XI, it was only disencumbered of canonical penalties as war broke out, by Pius XII.) In January 1946 Maritain, now French ambassador to the Holy See, had reported to Journet the disquiet at Rome about the intellectual tendencies in France, but thought the most the pope was likely to do would be to publish some kind of positive if rather platitudinous document about the nobility of speculative philosophy and theology and the need for Catholic thought to continue to draw inspiration from Thomas. But Père Réginald Garrigou-Lagrange, doyen of the *rigorissimi* Thomists of the Angelicum, and a highly active consultor of the Holy Office, seems to have expected more slapping down for the errant Jesuits when in June of that same year he confided to Nicolas that he personally had briefed the pope on Labourdette's forthcoming article; some weeks later, Pius XII sought out Maritain's own views on the matter. The pope's phrase "the new theology" may have been fed him by Garrigou, though this is not certain,[16] and the highly negative interpretation put upon the phrase almost as soon as it was uttered depends in part on that (putative) link, for Garrigou had written in July 1946 to Labourdette calling Daniélou's "Orientations présentes" "the manifesto of this new theology... Here [at Rome] we are highly attentive to this movement, which is a return to Modernism".[17] De Lubac would deny that the phrase "*nova theologia*" was at this stage intended as an attack on him and his collaborators. In his *Mémoires sur l'occasion de mes livres*, he notes how at a Castel Gandolfo audience during the course of the Jesuit gathering, the pope had said to him in friendly, not threatening, fashion, "Je connais votre doctrine", and the Jesuit General, when the Congregation was over, confirmed with both the Holy Office and Pius XII himself that de Lubac was well considered.[18]

Both inside the Society and outside matters looked different. Journet told Fessard that the object of the pope's remarks was virtually the same as the group lambasted by the *Revue Thomiste*. Yet the claim that the *nouvelle théologie* was Modernism *redivivus* was not one Labourdette had ever made. The reply of the incriminated Jesuits was published at the behest of the Roman authorities of the Society, and widely diffused in offprinted form. As de Lubac admitted in a letter of 1988 to the Italian historian of theology Antonio Russo, he himself was the main author of the anonymous "Réponse" which went out through the pages of the premier French Jesuit journal *Recherches de science religieuse* for 1946 – though he had enjoyed assistance from Daniélou,

---

[16] A. Russo, *Henri de Lubac: Teologia e dogma nella storia. L'influsso di Blondel* (Rome 1990), pp. 145-146. De Lubac had himself used it in the first part of *Surnaturel* which, despatched to the censors in August 1941, had received a *nihil obstat* in May 1942. Also, *L'Osservatore Romano* for 9-10 February 1942, in an article by the future cardinal Pietro Parente, had attacked "nuove tendenze teologiche" emanating from France.

[17] Letter of 17 July 1946, cited DT, p. 170.

[18] H. de Lubac, S. J., *Mémoires sur l'occasion de mes livres* (Namur 1989), pp. 62-63.

Bouillard, Fessard and Balthasar. Typical of de Lubac in polemical mood is the abrasive tone apparent in, for instance, the comment that, "If the evil days of Modernism are now, thank God, far from us, the evil days of integrism may be coming back".[19] Its main point, however, was simply to rebut without necessarily refuting the charge of historical and doctrinal relativism. The authors targeted by the Toulouse Dominicans, so readers were assured, show not the slightest trace of historicism whereas – taking the war into the enemy's country - a certain Scholastic theology possesses the contrary vice in its own thorough insensitivity to history. The Jesuit writers maligned by the Dominicans for incipient irrationalism rejoice in the rôle of the mind, and not just the heart, in theology, but they fear – not without reason when looking at some products of Scholasticism – the perversion of intelligence into intellectualism.

> Catholic truth will always exceed its own conceptual expression, and even more so, therefore, its scientific formulation in an organised system.[20]

What the Church needs, its authors conclude, is "freedom for theological schools within a single orthodoxy". What she does not at all need, or deserve, is the willed imposition of some particular system of thought in the name of the faith as a whole. Other than this, the anonymous Jesuits refused to enter into any further debate.

If they supposed they would end the affair by such a sharp rebuke they were sadly mistaken. In February 1947 the pot boiled over. In that journal of the "petite Rome" of Switzerland, *Liberté de Fribourg*, the prestigious Polish Dominican logician Innozent Bocheński spoke of the new theology as a radical evolutionism and irrationalism which would warm up the tired remains of Modernism. Garrigou-Lagrange then dropped his "atom bomb", the article "La nouvelle théologie, où va-t-elle?" in the pages of

---

[19] Cited in DT, p. 174.
[20] Cited in DT, p. 172.

Angelicum.[21] And if his answer to his own question (Where is the new theology going?) was "Back to Modernism", he also knew where it had come from: the French lay philosopher Maurice Blondel's fateful definition of truth in his masterwork *L'Action* not as *adequatio rei et intellectus*, the correspondence of reality and mind, but *adequatio vitae et mentis*, the correspondence of mind with *life*.[22] It was perfectly true that Bouillard, as general editorial secretary of *Théologie*, had defined the aim of the latter as

> to draw Christian doctrine from its own wellsprings, and to find in it the truth of our life.[23]

Meanwhile, the election of Nicolas as provincial of Toulouse ensured that Labourdette's hands were not going to be tied from above. Indeed, Nicolas judged an immediate reply to the Jesuit "Réponse" to be a necessity for the defence of the Dominican understanding of the vocation of Thomism – all the more so, as he explained to Labourdette, in that having just returned from a meeting on missionary effort in France at L'Arbresle, the study house of the Province of Lyons (the meeting in question was of enormous importance in the gestation of the worker priest movement and the crisis in relations between the French Church and Rome which it precipitated) he could well believe that flight from doctrinal and theological truth might be the pattern of the

---

[21] Garrigou was keenly alert to Blondel's influence: thus his "La Notion pragmatiste de la vérité et ses conséquences en théologie", in *Acta Pontificiae Academiae S. Thomae Aquinatis IX* (1944), pp. 153-178. That is an important key to his "La nouvelle théologie où ou va-t-elle?", *Angelicum* (1946), pp. 126-145. See also B. de Solages, "Pour l'honneur de la théologie, les contre-sens du R. P. Garrigou-Lagrange", *Bulletin de littérature ecclésiastique* 2 (1947), pp. 65-84.

[22] Certainly Bouillard was heavily indebted to Blondel: see his "L'intention fondamentale de Maurice Blondel et la théologie", *Recherches de science religieuse* 36 (1949), pp. 321-402; idem., "Maurice Blondel et la théologie", ibid., 37 (1950), pp. 105-112, and his full length study, *Blondel et le Christianisme* (Paris 1961). For Bouillard's own work, useful is K. H. Neufeld, "Fundamentaltheologie in gewandelter Welt: Henri Bouillards theologische Beitrag", *Zeitschrift für katholische Theologie* 3 (1978), pp. 417-440. As to de Lubac, one student can write, "Blondel more than any other is the author to whom de Lubac repeatedly sends us back", A. Russo, *Henri de Lubac* (Cinisella Balsamo 1993), p. 10.

[23] Cited H. de Lubac, *Mémoires sur l'occasion de mes livres, op. cit.*, p. 29.

future. All the Dominicans of Saint-Maximin, the intelligentsia of the Toulouse Province, were convinced that the line taken by the Lyons Jesuits, if widely followed, would spell disaster for the fortunes of Thomism in the Church. Where they differed was only on the question of whether it was right or appropriate to seek the arbitration of the Roman magisterium. The refusal to print the Garrigou article in the pages of the *Revue Thomiste* amounted to a decision not to pursue the notion of a Roman intervention – a decision which, Labourdette prophesied, would place them between two millstones where they would be crushed simultaneously from right (the Angelicum of Garrigou, the Catholic University at Angers, and Solesmes, the influential and highly conservative Benedictine Congregation of France), and from left (Cardinal Saliège, the Institut Catholique de Toulouse, and de Lubac).

This did not mean, however, that Labourdette and Nicolas would soften their line, as became plain when their response to the *Réponse* saw the light of day in May 1947.[24] They maintained that the metaphysics of St Thomas are, quite simply, true, not just as an hypothesis or as the expression of a mentality but objectively and by the nature of things. Moreover, they claimed of Thomism that it was not only a theology of nature and essence but also a theology of event and therefore in a real sense a theology of history; they accepted that theology is not revelation, and however perfect it may be leaves open spaces which premature appeal to the magisterium ought not to foreclose; they state nonetheless that they cannot be regarded as mere partisans, for Thomism is not a party but the philosophy and theology of the Church herself – even if what is most profoundly at stake in the present quarrel is not the rights of the doctrine of St Thomas so much as those of theology itself when considered as a veridical science of God and his relation with the world.

It was Labourdette who had given the most eloquent expression to this view, not only in "La théologie et ses sources"

---

[24] M. -M. Labourdette, O. P. - M. J. Nicolas, O. P., "L'analogie de la Vérité et l'unité de la Science théologique", *Revue Thomiste* 55 (1947), pp. 417-466.

but also in a programmatic statement, "La théologie, intelligence de la foi", which had preceded the essay on the sources of theology in the January/March 1946 issue of the *Revue Thomiste*.[25] Labourdette feared that in the future there might be historians of the thought of St Thomas, curators of a Thomist museum, but not actual disciples of Thomas. An excessive or, worse, an exclusive delight in historical truth was, he held, an obstacle to any mind desirous of an integral intellectual development. Erudition can cease to be at the service of thought and transform itself into a pretext for refusing the question of truth: what Aquinas himself had called *curiositas*. It is not enough to be an historical theologian, to know how problems were posed in the past One must have an answer to them now. Nor is there any need to cobble together a new philosophy and theology for this purpose for one already exists that can do the job. The Thomist synthesis is essentially true in its principles; though imperfect, it is, therefore, eminently perfectible by contemporary and future effort. Better than anyone before him Thomas grasped the foundational truths of metaphysics and how to build on them a synthesis which would be all the more hospitable to every truth precisely because dependent on a true metaphysic. The essential task of Thomas's disciples is to integrate into this truth all newly discovered truth, including nuggets of truth occurring in philosophical and theological systems otherwise false, and this requires both critical vigilance and constructive effort. But in and of themselves, the other systems – Scotist or Hegelian, Existentialist or evolutionist – are irreconcilable with Thomism and so one has to choose. Labourdette stressed that Thomism was not an eclectic product but a structured organism thanks to those theological and metaphysical principles, universal in their bearing, which had allowed it to assimilate and turn into wisdom what was best in the traditions which preceded it. Thus, while rejecting a "fixisme" which would look only to the letter of St Thomas's texts (such a policy would contradict the demands of theological research and

---

[25] [M. -M. Labourdette], "La théologie, intelligence de la foi", *Revue Thomiste XLVI* 1 (1946), pp. 5-44.

the spirit of Thomism itself, as well as leading to the inevitable extinction of the latter as a living system), he also spurned a "mobilisme" which would conceive the history of theology as the continuous substitution of systems and schemes in dependence on what struck people as better adapted to current needs or present day intellectual styles. The idea that what one should take from Thomas, for example, is the spirit of openness which led him to welcome the work of Aristotle, Labourdette stigmatised as a "sottise" which betrays a zero understanding of what theology is. Thomism cannot just be a state of mind of openness to modernity since by itself this does not answer the question as to what doctrinal, philosophical and theological principles could make such an openness fruitful precisely for the Christian faith.

Labourdette emphasised with particular vigour that the prime value of Thomism does not reside first and foremost in this or that thesis proposed by Thomas, but in the fact that Thomism realises the complete idea of what theology should be, "la notion intégrale de la théologie".[26] This is what enabled the Toulouse Thomists to claim that their struggle was not for Thomas *qua* Thomas, but for theology itself – for that intellectual enterprise which would think through the corpus of Christian doctrine on the basis of soundly established metaphysical first principles. Everyone can agree that theology is faith seeking understanding, but St Anselm's is only a minimum definition of the task. There is no theology properly so called until this understanding of the faith has constituted itself as a science, culminating in a speculative synthesis – at one and the same time the matured fruit of contemplation and yet something capable of being taught to others. Such a speculative synthesis, Labourdette thought, should aim to reproduce in the human mind, and so in a human way, the totality of what is given to us through both natural understanding and divine revelation in that totality's own intelligible structure. This and this alone explains why St Thomas calls theology at its highest, *quaedam impressio divinae scientiae*, "a kind of impression

---

[26] S.-T. Bonino, O. P., "Le Thomisme du P. Labourdette", in MT, p. 95.

of the divine knowledge".[27] In the thirteenth century there took place a providential encounter of the true religion with the true philosophy, and the faith of the Church Fathers, which hitherto had not found its proper conceptual instrument, now had this within its grasp. Though much in historic Aristotelianism had to be re-thought by Christian theologians, the idea of attempting to go behind the "Thomist miracle" to any understanding of the faith typical of an earlier epoch is inadmissible, a betrayal of theology's very essence.

For Labourdette, the study of the Christian mystery via the ruminations of the Fathers is not, *senso strictu*, theology. But then, for him, theology is not the whole of Christian thought. Theology, though, can only play its part within the wider corpus of Christian thinking and contribute effectively to the Church's life if it jealously preserves its own specificity – which is that of a sacred *science*, faithful to its own needs and methods, and not to those identified by pastoral surveys or general intellectual history.

By the summer of 1947 (to return to the *déroulement* of the drama), the French episcopate had begun to express anxiety about the negative effect the entire debate was having on the Church's image among unbelievers. Labourdette replied that, fortunately for the faith, such public relations considerations had not been the primary preoccupation of St Athanasius. In their own correspondence, the Jesuits concerned ridiculed the Dominicans as intellectually second rate. Surely, wrote de Lubac, their time would be better spent in choir. Nicolas came to fear, as he wrote to Garrigou, that before crossing swords with such men it would have been advantageous to enjoy an intellectual culture equal to their own.

By Easter 1947, Saint-Maximin was ready to extend an olive branch, and Labourdette wrote an eirenic piece conceding the liberty of the various theological schools but not their parity.[28] The Roman Dominicans considered its somewhat contrite tone uncalled for. They need not have feared the too facile triumph of

---

[27] *Summa Theologiae*, Ia., q. 1, a. 3, ad ii.
[28] "Fermes propos", *Revue Thomiste* 47 (1947), pp. 5-19.

those who cry peace where there is no peace since insufficient mutual good will was forthcoming to create a real reconciliation though many tried – most ambitiously the Oratorian and convert from Calvinism Louis Bouyer who, together with the Jesuit Plotinus scholar Paul Henry, wanted to secure the signatures of all the leading Catholic intellectuals in France to a common statement on the inter-relation of revelation, dogma and theology.

In 1950 Pius XII issued his encyclical *Humani Generis*, a critique of certain errors in modern thought, and owing to complaisance in these, of displeasing tendencies in current philosophy and theology in the Catholic schools. "We are satisfied" (the pope wrote):

> that Catholic teachers in general keep clear of these errors, but it is certain that there are others, now as in the time of the apostles, who have too ready an ear for novelties."[29]

But who did this cap fit? Some conservative theologians, after all, were disappointed at the encyclical's comparative moderation and the pope's refusal to issue condemnations of named writers – even of the highly exposed Teilhard de Chardin. Alerted by the Saint-Maximin controversy, the Jesuit authorities were sure it must at least fit Bouillard and de Lubac, who were consequently deprived of their teaching rôles. By de Lubac's own account, the pope had changed his good opinion of him of three years earlier, interrupting cardinal Gerlier of Lyons when the latter defended him with the words, "The trouble with him is that you never know whether what he says or writes corresponds to what he is thinking". The most discussed of the various works arraigned in "La théologie et ses sources" – "Orientations présentes" at their head – were removed from the open shelves of Jesuit libraries. To the French Jesuits thus treated, the events of 1950 and the years following were a monstrous nightmare: in their eyes, the true "nouvelle théologie" was the late Scholasticism defended *à l'outrance* by Garrigou and with much more nuance by

---

[29] *Humani Generis*, 10. See G. Weigel, "The Historical Background of the Encyclical *Humani Generis*", *Theological Studies* 12 (1951), pp. 208-230, and idem., "Gleanings from the Commentaries on *Humani Generis*", ibid., 12 (1951), pp. 520-549.

Labourdette. *This* was the upstart theology alien not only to the Fathers but to the thirteenth century golden age itself. That was the point at issue with de Lubac's study of the relation between human nature and the vision of God in his *Surnaturel* – by 1950 the most controverted contribution to the series *Théologie*, though its appearance in the summer of 1946 had been too tardy for it to receive notice in the Labourdette essay.

Ignorant of all the relevant facts, Congar accused Labourdette of "arming the infernal machine"[30] – meaning the machinery which, somewhere in the recesses of the *Curia romana*, had coerced the Jesuit generalate into taking such action. In fact, Labourdette had genuinely desired not condemnation but dialogue. In a fashion psychologically easy to envisage, he found himself disabled for the future from very much in the way of critical animadversion on the direction Church and theological life were taking. Hence, despite the reservations expressed in his diary for the Second Vatican Council's first session, he rallied to the Conciliar majority at the beginning of Paul VI's pontificate. (Not that this would save him in the post-1968 era.)

For Thomism, the vindication by the Council of the maligned directors of *Sources Chrétiennes* and *Théologie* was, in all the circumstances, not the best of news. For contrary to Labourdette's intention, the fatal impression had been given that recourse to the Fathers, to Church history, and to contemporary thought are scarcely compatible with a firm adhesion to the Thomist patrimony. And so the victory for those who represented the patristic revival, a better informed theology, and a pastorally motivated interest in contemporary thought could only appear as the defeat of Thomism itself. Some words of Père Marie-Dominique Chenu, around the time of the crisis, proved prophetic. Writing à propos of Bouyer's *Mystère Paschal,* just published, he remarked in May 1945, by way of reference to the four movements of theological renewal – the biblical, the liturgical, the spiritual and the apostolic:

---

[30] DT, p. 193, paraphrasing letters of 4 and 8 November 1949 and 1 February 1952 in the Papiers Congar.

> In the measure that we, the professionals of Scholasticism, ...
> close ourselves to this fourfold renewal, we shall lose both
> Scholasticism itself and contact with the life of the Spirit.[31]

But the crucial question was, How is the relation of Thomism
with such return to 'the sources and the dialogue with
contemporary thought to be mediated? This was the real question
raised by Labourdette but never squarely answered. The issue of
the legitimate pluralism of Catholic philosophy and theology, and
yet the unique place to be accorded to the classical speculative
thought of St Thomas and his continuators[32] within this charmed
circle remains as actual and unresolved today as in the years when
the events I have tried to describe unfolded.

Some brief indications of the direction of a possible answer
may be appended. Because "to be" is the most foundational of all
words expressive of the real, a metaphysics of being has to provide
the basic grammar for a theology that would do justice to the truth
of reality. A theology that thinks through the materials of divine
revelation in this perspective must therefore enjoy a primacy
among the various possible intellectual adventures that issue from
the act of faith. Let us call it "the classical ontological theology",
which, historically, is deeply indebted to if not exactly co-
terminous with Thomas and his school.

But not all theologies have this aim. They may, like that of
Denys in the ancient Church, seek in the context of the spiritual,
cosmic and sacramental order of the Church, to bring about our
mystical return to the One, or, in the modern Church, like
Balthasar's, try to express the supreme beauty of the Gospel and its
unsurpassable dramatic power. Such theologies are hardly in
competition with the classical ontological theology. Indeed, they

---

[31] Letter of 23 March 1945, cited DT, p. 159.

[32] In the Dominican Constitutions Labourdette would have studied as a novice at
Saint-Maximin, we read:

> the solid doctrine of St Thomas – which our Order proposes and orders our
> brothers to follow – is not only that which is expressed without any doubt in
> the works of the angelic doctor, but also that which is taught by his school;
> thus called because it manifests the thought of that doctor.

Constitutions, S. O. P., ed. L. Theissling (Rome 1925), no. 26, p. 261.

would suffer from its diminution since, if they are orthodox, they depend upon it (knowingly or not, because its full articulation may occur at a point subsequent to their own historical moment) for the metaphysical presuppositions of their own catholicity. Those presuppositions the Church has recognised as required by the biblical revelation (to which all theologies are tributary) in sanctioning the classical ontological theology itself.

The Toulouse Dominicans were right, therefore, to claim as much as they did for Thomas, but wrong in allowing so little *droit de cité* to the *nouvelle théologie*. It is not the case that, grudgingly, the other theologies are permitted to exist until Thomism has absorbed their better insights (whereupon, like the Marxist State, they can wither away), though Thomism certainly should absorb what it can from them consonant with its own proper aim. Rather is it the case that their differing theological functions should be honoured so long as these other theologies define their functions in a way that leaves the irreplaceable rôle of the classical ontological theology intact. This is the twist I would give to the commendation of Scholasticism in *Humani Generis*: "No surer way to safeguard the first principles of the faith and turn the results of later, healthy developments to good advantage".[33]

---

[33] *Humani Generis*, 31.

III

A VIEW FROM COLOGNE: THE FATE OF PATRISTIC TRINITARIANISM IN MODERN CATHOLIC THEOLOGY

We are familiar with the notion that, in sacred studies in the Catholic context (but by no means exclusively there), the present century has been characterised by a series of movements of *ressourcement* – *recursus ad fontes*, "going back to the sources" – of which the most important were the biblical, liturgical and patristic revivals. It has been noted, sometimes acerbically, that the movement of patristic *ressourcement* owes something to the difficulties encountered by its elder sister, the biblical renewal in the course of the Modernist crisis. If one feared one would fall foul of Church authority by practising the higher criticism after the manner of the Universities of Berlin or Jena, one might well prefer as an alternative to edit a fifth century chronicle of the pious practices of monks. (That was the origin, for instance, of Dom Cuthbert Butler's presentation of Palladius's *Lausiac History*.) But, that apart, historians of theology have been content to map the massive fact of this and other returns to the sources without too much enquiry into their causes. The "massive fact" was chiefly of interest to them as a way of explaining the passing of neo-Scholastic hegemony in Catholic church-culture at the time of the Second Vatican Council. The massiveness in question also obscured from view the very real presence of the Fathers, not least as Trinitarian thinkers, in the theology of the nineteenth century, whether in the Roman or other schools. And since I am keen not to perpetuate the illusion that, before the movements of *ressourcement*, theology wandered in a barren landscape "ethnically cleansed" of all traces of the Fathers' blessed race, I would like to launch an account of the fate of patristic Trinitarianism in modern Catholic dogmatics from the pad of the late nineteenth century. What I want to show is how things could be done then, and what questions, hesitations or re-evaluations vis-à-vis the role of patristic theses in speculative theology have emerged since. The writer I shall take as my *point de repère* is a rewarding one: Matthias Joseph Scheeben, now an unjustly neglected figure in the English-speaking world.[1]

Writing as an historically well-informed Scholastic divine at the seminary of Cologne, Scheeben gives forty-three pages out of one hundred and sixty of his tractate on the Holy Trinity in the *Handbuch der katholischen Dogmatik* to a consideration of the patristic treatment of the subject, prior to entering upon his own distinctive understanding of what he calls "the genetic development of the Trinity from out of the fruitfulness of the divine life".[2] A brisk canter through the ante-Nicene Fathers and writers produces the following conclusion. Although the content of authentic Trinitarian understanding was "to hand" in the consciousness of believers, and *a fortiori* of Catholic Fathers and teachers (that can be known from the prolegomena to dogmatics in the theology of revelation and its transmission, thus licensing a benign interpretation of the historical data), neither the fundamental truths of Trinitarian believing nor their further implications came to expression so sharply and aptly as would later be the case. The weaknesses were these. The Father's character as Source and Principle was so strongly stressed as to make it appear as if he alone were God *simpliciter*, Son and Spirit being divine only by virtue of communion, *Gemeinschaft*, with the Father and in less perfect fashion. In an effort to avoid ditheism, a full affirmation of the identity in substance of the Father and a divine Other was not forthcoming; instead people spoke of a substantial relationship, merely, or even of a simple communion in the Father's power or authority, action, love or unity. Next, in an effort to extricate the Father from any subordination to blind or coercive necessity, the generation of the Son was described as

---

[1] But see my "Homage to Scheeben", in A. Nichols, O. P., *Scribe of the Kingdom: Essays on Theology and Culture*, op. cit., I. pp. 205-213.

[2] M. J. Scheeben, *Handbuch der katholischen Dogmatik*, I (Freiburg 1874; 1933), pp. 795-838 on the Fathers; 839-906 on Scheeben's own *intellectus fidei*.

voluntary – though Scheeben allows that this term *can* bear a proper meaning in that context, hence its survival among orthodox writers *after* Nicaea.[3] A related difficulty is that, misled by Proverbs 8 where Wisdom cries, "The Lord created me at the beginning of his work" (v. 22), the Son's generation can appear as ordered to the world's creation, perhaps in the mitigated form of the concept of a twofold generation, in eternity and in time. The final weakness of ante-Nicene Trinitarianism for Scheeben is that it tends to locate the *distinctivum* of the Father, what will later be called his hypostatic particularity, in an inappropriate place – namely, his invisibility as Sender of Son and Spirit who alone appear visibly, under sensuous forms and symbols.

In seeking to show how the doctrinal tradition was so consolidated as to make available a sound dogmatic grasp of the mystery for further exploration by a speculative dogmatician such as Scheeben aims to be, the Cologne theologian is extremely even-handed in the laurels he awards to East and West His account of how these lacunae in pre-Nicene writing were successfully filled divides up into eighteen pages on the Greek Fathers (mostly Athanasius and Basil) and sixteen on the Latin – though here the need to deal with the *Filioque* issue produces references in passing to Maximus and Damascene. Still, this parity of pages should not deceive us. Not for nothing does Scheeben's exposition of the Greek-speaking writers come first, for these are the principal architects of that two-story dogmatic building, Nicaea and Constantinople. Scheeben considers that this preferential option, in the order of exposition, for the East does not in any way prevent – indeed he thinks, it licenses – the giving of primacy to the unity of the divine substance. What Athanasius witnessed to was precisely the communication of the entire substance of the Begetter to the Begotten so that both possess one and the same divine being. What Basil argued against the Eunomians was that, as between the divine life of Begotten and Begetter, the only difference is that it is in the first case a life that is *received*, and in

---

[3] For the case of Gregory Nazianzen, see A. Nichols, O. P., *Byzantine Gospel: Maximus the Confessor in Modern Scholarship* (Edinburgh 1993), pp. 72-73.

the second case, not. The unity of essence of Father, Son and Spirit, remarks Scheeben, with acknowledgement to Athanasius, again, and Nazianzen, is the "unity of a substantial and indivisible continuity (*Zusammenhang*), of coherence and inseparability".[4] If such unity is compared by these Fathers with the immanent inherence of qualities, powers and activities in created spirits, that is not to be taken, they insist, as though the Persons proceeding are accidents of the Father's substance, for they are that very substance itself. The Persons' perfect reciprocal *Ineinandersein*, "in-one-another-ness", is not just spiritual co-presence, such as different beings might enjoy with each other, for it is included in the very concept of their total *homoousia*, and so is the condition and ground, not the consequence, of their personal acting.

All of that explains how the Greek Fathers can call the Trinity the "Monad" or the "Henad", and say of the divine Essence that it is one not just in the arithmetic sense which would imply some kind of counting within a possible series but in the more significant sense that no second or third positing of the divine nature is possible. Here Scheeben co-opts Athanasius and the Cappadocians into supporting the option of Latin theology since the High Middle Ages to treat the unity of the Three first. As the American Dominican William Hill has put it in what is perhaps from the Catholic side the most distinguished English-language work on Trinitarian theology in the last two decades:

> The justification for this order [oneness, then threeness] rather than the reverse is simply that God's identity can only be approached by way of analogy with what prevails in the world of creatures. There, the concept of unity enjoys a logical priority over multiplicity; it is possible to grasp things in their plurality only on the basis of first being aware of the unity of each of those entities that go to make up that unity.

But as Hill cautions:

---

[4] M. J. Scheeben, *Handbuch der katholischen Dogmatik* I, op. cit., p. 805.

This is not, of course, an order within God but solely an order
of intelligibility for a mind that thinks rationally; thus, the
theologian who proceeds this way must constantly bear in
mind that the God who is One in being *is* three Persons.[5]

That is a re-assurance as to the propriety of the lay-out of
the Latin treatises on God the Triune which not all Catholic
dogmaticians, by the mid-twentieth century, would find wholly
satisfying: the name of the Innsbrück Jesuit, Karl Rahner, whose
small but influential essay on Trinitarian theology I shall be
mentioning later[6], comes at once to mind. Scheeben's own
defence of a prioritising of the single divine *ousia* is not however,
like Hill's, epistemological, a matter of how human minds work,
but, if the pun may be allowed, is more substantive. His most
telling point is that every manner of distinguishing the divine
Three would fall away if the unity of Essence were not first grasped
as so complete that the distinction of Persons arises precisely as *a*
difference in their possession of It, the condition of which is the
origin of One through relationship with the Others. For
Scheeben, the *monarchia* in the Holy Trinity lies in the Son and
Spirit being "out of" the Father with whom they have the selfsame
Essence. Both halves of this formula, the "personalist" and the
"essentialist", are to his mind indispensable in a proper statement
of the Monarchy.

Do we see at work here a spirit of integration and
equilibrium in the utilisation of patristic texts on the Trinity
which is imperilled by a one-sided attack on "essentialism" –
usually in the name of the highly particular reading of the
Cappadocian achievement associated with the Greek Orthodox
theologian, much read in Catholic circles, Bishop John Zizioulas?[7]
There can be such a thing as a unilateral personalism which is

---

[5] W. J. Hill, O. P., *The Three-Personed God: The Trinity as a Mystery of Salvation* (Washington 1982; 1988), pp. 256-257.

[6] K. Rahner, S. J., *The Trinity* (London and New York 1966). The German original is an essay, "Der dreifältige Gott als transzendente Urgrund der Heilsgeschichte", published in J. Feiner – Löhrer (eds.), *Mysterium Salutis* II/C (Einsiedeln 1967).

[7] J. Zizioulas, *Being as Communion* (Et Crestwood, N. Y., 1985).

barely distinguishable from a vitiated voluntarism as when Zizioulas portrays the Father as freely constituting his own essence. As a recent contributor to an Eastern Orthodox theological journal has noted, unless Son and Spirit are to be reduced to a level of secondary divinity here, "nature and essence cannot be emptied of content as much as Zizioulas would like". Speaking of both the relations of origin and those of communion, V. F. Harrison goes on:

> The essence remains ontologically dependent on the persons, as he takes care to affirm, but it serves as a medium, so to speak, through which the persons actualize their relatedness and freely offer themselves to each other... The common essence or nature is intrinsic to the relatedness which constitutes their existence, freedom and equality as persons.[8]

Perhaps more of Scheeben's space than in an ecumenically sensitive age we would consider altogether appropriate, is devoted to defending the view that the *Filioque*, understood, with the Council of Florence, in the sense of a *per Filium*, is the conviction of the Greek Fathers, before Photius, at large. Here too we anticipate somewhat another *crux* in the twentieth century Catholic reception of patristic Trinitarianism: whether, as for instance with Hans Urs von Balthasar, roundly to re-affirm – and indeed to glory in – the *Filioque* quite as much as, on the Eastern Orthodox side, a Vladimir Lossky might repudiate – and indeed excoriate – it; or, by contrast, to soften its force, as with the French "moine apostolique", strongly supported on this point by the Holy See, Jean-Miguel Garrigues; or again to find a formulation which circumvents the whole issue (no matter what may be said or sung while in church!), as with the American Capuchin Thomas Weinandy in his study *The Father's Spirit of Sonship*.[9] The proposal of that study, that it is by the power of the Spirit that the Father generates the Son, is prolonged in a French language work,

---

[8] V. F. Harrison, "Zizioulas on Communion and Otherness", *St Vladimir's Theological Quarterly* 42, 3-4 (1998), pp. 273-300. And here at pp. 279-280.

[9] T. G. Weinandy, O. F. M. Cap., *The Father's Spirit of Sonship: Reconceiving the Trinity* (Edinburgh 1992).

François-Xavier Durrwell's *Jésus, Fils de Dieu dans l'Esprit Saint,*[10] which draws the further inference that it is by the Spirit that the Father is Father and the Son Son – an example of the pendulum swinging so far from a supposed downplaying of pneumatology in the Western tradition as almost to leave the clock-case altogether. Scheeben, it is worth remarking, does not argue for the theological perspicuity of the *Filioque* notwithstanding the historically admitted fact that the Greek doctors by and large do not hold it (the position of, say, Balthasar or, on the Reformed side, Karl Barth). He maintains that the Greek doctors *do* hold it, for what they controverted with the Pneumatochians was the right understanding of the claim that the Holy Spirit goes out from the Son (not as do the gifts of creation and redemption, they argued, but as does One who is divine). Why, then, does the *Filioque* not appear in the Constantinopolitan Symbol? The simplest way to put forth a dogma which would defend the mystery of the Spirit's Godhead was to affirm his origin in the Father's substance. No shorter, more scriptural (compare John 15, First Corinthians 2) means to their end could be found than was this.

Is there then *no* perceptible difference between Eastern and Western Triadology in the patristic age as Scheeben sees it? Scheeben has already explained how in the Greek East speaking of the Spirit's procession *through* the Son was preferred to talk of his origin *from* Son and Father, and goes on to say that in some respects that formula is indeed objectively preferable. It is good biblical exegesis to say of the Son, as the Johannine Christ says of himself, that he is "the Way" – by which all comes from the Father and through which all returns to him. That median rôle is also the Son's in the spiration of the Spirit. And in any case the Father and Son are never *parallel* principles of anything. Rather are they *zwei ineinander wirkende Prinzipien,*[11] two circumcessively operative principles, and specifically in relation to the procession of the Spirit the Son is but *principium de principio*, a principle from a principle, as the Father enables him to co-spirate the Spirit in

---

[10] F. -X. Durrwell, Jésus, Fils de Dieu dans l'Esprit Saint (Paris 1997).
[11] M. J. Scheeben, *Handbuch der katholischen Dogmatik*, I. op. cit., p. 819.

giving him (the Son) in the eternal act of his generation all that is the Father's own. The *per Filium* attests the more organic quality of Eastern Triadology whereby the Begetting and the Breathing appear as one progressive movement from the Father, the second moment in "inner, essential and living continuity" with the first. (Here Scheeben anticipates Garrigues by noting how a richer Hellenic vocabulary for procession than Latin possesses can make the difference between the mediate and the ultimate origin of the Holy Spirit plain.) The Spirit goes forth from the Son only insofar as, thanks to his Sonship, the Son is and remains in the Father – that, for Scheeben, is a perfectly good "Greek" way of expressing the Latin conviction that Father and Son constitute one principle for the being of the Spirit. In the Latin tradition, which, contrary to the characterisations of many history of doctrine textbooks, Scheeben considers to be *more* personalist on this point, the procession of the Spirit is an act expressive of the personal communion which the Only Begotten Son enjoys with the Father by virtue of his unity and equality with him – such that (and this, says Scheeben, is already clear in Ambrose and Jerome, in other words, the dread name of St Augustine need not yet appear!) the Spirit is the bond and pledge, which rhyme nicely in German, *Band und Pfand*, of their mutual love. Nothing could be more suitable, in this context, to say of the Spirit that he proceeds *ex Patre et Filio*. We are dealing here, Scheeben believed, not with a contradiction in patristic pluralism, but a complementariness.

Does the reiterated emphasis on the Holy Spirit as *vinculum amoris*, the bond of love of Father and Son, lead to his seeming irrelevant to the Trinitarian economy in the world, and indeed to the occlusion of his being as a Person – theses strongly maintained by the United Reformed Church theologian Professor Colin Gunton of King's College, London, not without some influence on Catholic students of things Trinitarian? The French Jesuit Bertrand de Margerie has pointed out that, for Augustine, the goal of the relations of divine Persons with human is always so to manifest the divine to the human that the human may participate in the divine. When in Book XV of the *De Trinitate* Augustine in effect applies this principle to the mission of the Spirit as the Trinitarian "bond of love", the connexion with our own salvation is transparent. In the words of the African doctor:

> According to the Sacred Scriptures, the Holy Spirit is neither of the Father alone nor of the Son alone, but of both of them: and thus he instils in us the common charity by which the Father and the Son mutually love each other.[12]

The Spirit is thus the bond of inner-ecclesial communion by being the bond of communion of Christians with the Father and the Son.

Before leaving the topic of the *Filioque* we can observe how Scheeben, in an inverted mirror-image of what will be Lossky's position, deals with Filioquism's antithesis, the Monopatrism of the patriarch Photius. As the schism with the Chalcedonian Orthodox in the East is the most disastrous of all schisms, he says, so we must expect the heresy which catalysed it to be the worst of all heresies, for it introduces schism into God himself, destroying the "economy" in God (here Scheeben is using the word *economia* in its Tertullianic, not its Irenaean which is also its later sense) by denying the "life-filled unity and relationship" between the Spirit and the Father's Son – just as the denial of the Son's visible representative on earth (Scheeben means, of course, the Roman pope) destroys the *oikonomia* of the Church. The presiding in love of the first see (the reference is to Ignatius's Letter to the Romans) is spurned precisely because of the *Filioque* which denotes the "most perfect and glorious Ideal and Source of loving communion, *Liebesgemeinschaft*" – the Spirit's breathing forth as reciprocal affection of Father and Son.[13]

So far we have heard little if anything of *hypostases* or "persons", terminology whose contemporary suitability has been widely discussed in mid- and later twentieth century Catholic dogmatics, where a revival of the language of "modes of subsistence", itself indebted to the Cappadocians, again, has been

---

[12] B. de Margerie, S. J., *The Christian Trinity in History* (Et Petersham, Mass. 1982) pp. xxi, 114-121; Augustine, *De Trinitate*, XV. 17, 27.
[13] M. J. Scheeben, *Handbuch der katholischen Dogmatik*, I, op. cit., p. 825.

both lauded and deplored. For Scheeben, recourse to an abstract vocabulary conceptually indicative of the ontological status of Father, Son and Holy Spirit in precisely their distinctness was forced on the Church once the conviction had found adequate articulation that the divine Three share the self-same Essence or *ousia*. Otherwise, simply to have continued to speak, with biblical concreteness, of Spirit, Son and Father would have sufficed, and sublimely sufficed at that. With considerable metaphysical refinement, Scheeben builds up for his readers the idea of hypostasis as substance that is singular rather than apportioned to some wider whole, so standing in its own right that its properties are really its own, the bearer of its nature. And when the nature in question is spiritual – *geistig* – nature, the hypostasis is not simply the bearer – *Träger* – of that nature but its *Inhaber* – intimate possessor, consciously enjoying that nature and freely making use of it in such a way as to own a dignity that is alien to animals, and much more so to things. Scheeben evidently believed it was possible to use the word "person", in the context of rational creatures, for a subjectivity that is of a metaphysical order, without importing irrelevant considerations drawn from human psychology. The preference for the language of "modes of subsistence" or some variant thereof shown by Karl Rahner derives from a conviction that "three persons" could now only mean "three psyches", the Church having no power, alas, to determine the fluctuations of human language. That is not to say, of course, that calling Father, Son and Holy Spirit *Subsistenz-weisen* is without its difficulties. As Rahner's Canadian confrère Bernard Lonergan drily comments in his *De Deo trino*, "Non enim cum modis essendi collequi solemus", "It is not our habit to enter into dialogue with modes of being".[14] For Scheeben, the concept of created personhood, philosophically purified, forms an entirely suitable starting-point for the analogical predication of uncreated personhood to the divine Three. Personhood is a created perfection in being which can be ascribed in a super-eminent

---

[14] B. Lonergan, S. J., *De Deo trino* (Rome 1964), II., p. 195; cited in B. de Margerie, S.J., *The Christian Trinity in History*, op. cit., p. 215.

fashion to the uncreated way of being of Father, Son and Spirit. This is how Scheeben takes the Cappadocians to have understood the divine hypostases as *tropoi tês hyparxeôs*, ways of subsisting, of the divine *ousia*. The hypostases are the divine *ousia*, in a special form – the tri-personal form – of its self-belonging.

It was Scheeben's opinion that the difference between Greek East and Latin West in the matter of the origin of the Spirit betokens a wider difference here, where the relation of the hypostases one with another is seen more organically in the East, more personally – that is, involving an inter-personal exchange – in the West. For that the divine Persons are persons in the highest sense of the word does not exclude but on the contrary includes the consideration that they are essentially relative to one another, such that they possess the divine nature only insofar as each has it for another or from another. Such a patristically-inspired vision might be thought to appeal to twentieth century men and women who, in the idiom, part philosophical, part psychological of their time, delight to speak of selfhood as found in relation – a paraphrase, that, of the title of a work by a philosopher of Presbyterian background, John MacMurray, that has influenced Anglophone Catholics writing on anthropology in the last few decades. But even when couched in such terms there are those, among them the recently deceased American lay theologian Catherine LaCugna, for whom all talk of God's self-relatedness as Trinity, however expressed, is in evangelical bad taste. [15] For these writers, it is not simply that the economic Trinity is the immanent Trinity *and vice versa* (as Rahner's book, already mentioned, had averred), thus deliberately suppressing all talk of the divine condescension in the way the Trinitarian missions prolong the Trinitarian processions. More than this, any mention of the immanent Trinity must be eliminated as lacking congruity with the revelation of a God who is essentially *outpoured* in creation and salvation into the world. Here we have the Catholic version of the

---

[15] C. M. LaCugna, *God for Us: The Trinity and Christian Life* (New York 1991): note the claim on p. 15 that "Revealed [in the economy] is the unfathomable mystery that the life and communion of the divine persons is not 'intradivine'".

Neo-economic Trinitarianism of the Lutheran Jürgen Moltmann though minus the latter's Hegelian underpinning for which it is only in the economy – specifically on the Cross – that God fully becomes Trinity at all.

What is at stake here, I would say, is a failure of doxological thinking where we exult precisely in the glorious objectivity of God, his divinity, which means for Christianity, his triunity, just for its own sake. This was not a burden under which Scheeben laboured. In his account of the divine self-relating, a divine Person is the divine Essence under a determinate relation, such that to name the Persons is to name the relations – a realisation for which we are indebted, says Scheeben, to Augustine's *De Trinitate* (I, 7) though we should note how sparing is the appeal to that treatise in Scheeben's account of Trinitarian doctrine: Augustine's explorations of the processions on the analogy of the production of spiritual understanding and love belong for him firmly to theological speculation, rather than dogma. In the mid- to late twentieth century, that subject has entered an interesting phase: on the one hand we have rather self-consciously orthodox theologians such as the Belgian Jesuit, Jean Galot, professor at the Gregorianum, preparing to dispense with the Augustinian (and Thomistic) account of the two inter-related acts of intelligence and will as too defective an analogy, for the Trinitarian processions for the Son cannot be conceived as generated without love, nor the Spirit of holiness "reduced to love alone".[16] On the other hand, the discovery of historical theologians that the selfsame analogy pervades the Trinitarianism of St Gregory Palamas should make pause those who would dismiss it as a superfluous Augustinian-Thomistic peculiarity, for both Catholic and Orthodox students have seen Palamas (the first negatively, the second positively) as embodying what is least typically Latin in the later Byzantine doctrine of God.[17] Still, since the *intra*-subjective comparison of

---

[16] J. Galot, S. J., *L'Esprit-Saint: Personne de communion* (Saint-Maur 1997).

[17] R. Flogaus, "Palamas and Barlaam Revisited: A Re-assessment of East and West in the Hesychast Controversy of 14th Century Byzantium", *St Vladimir's Theological*

the self and its spiritual acts is simply an image of the Trinity, there is no reason why theologians should not seek complementary images of a more *inter*-subjective kind, as when Bertrand de Margerie would revive Nazianzen's Trinitarian image of family inter-subjectivity in the *Fifth Theological Oration*, and Augustine's account of ecclesial inter-subjectivity – the universal Church as icon of the triune God, in not only the *De Trinitate* but also the *Tractates on John*.[18]

I cannot conclude without painting into my picture what has recently been deemed the single most striking common feature of much contemporary Catholic dogmatic writing on the Holy Trinity – namely, the way that subject is treated in close connexion with the Paschal Mystery.[19] The mystery of the Atonement not only redeems, it also reveals – and above all it reveals the triune Source of our salvation. Here the work of Hans Urs von Balthasar is especially notable, but one can also mention two Frenchmen, the Spiritan Père Durrwell, whose name has already figured in my account and the Benedictine, Dom Ghislain Lafont. Here again, we can take our bearings from Cologne, for Scheeben lays a foundation for these later theologies in his doctrine of the redemptive Sacrifice as disclosure of the Trinity. As he puts it in *Die Mysterien des Christentums*, "The idea of Christ's sacrifice thrusts its roots deep into the abyss of the Trinity". Just as the Incarnation is intelligible only as the prolongation of the eternal generation of the Son, and must be grasped from that viewpoint, so the Son's sacrificial surrender on Calvary was the perfect expression of the love he manifests in the spiration from the Father of the Spirit. As he writes:

> In the Godhead the mutual love of the Son and the Father pours itself out in the production of the Holy Spirit, who issues from their common heart, in whom both surrender their heart's blood, and to whom they give themselves as the

---

Quarterly 42, 1 (1998), pp. 1-32. I am grateful to Mr Augustine Casiday of the University of Durham for drawing this article to my attention.
[18] B. de Margerie, *The Christian Trinity in History*, op. cit., pp. 274-297.
[19] A. Hunt, *The Trinity and the Paschal Mystery: A Development in Recent Catholic Theology* (Collegeville, Minn. 1997).

pledge of their infinite love ... Since the Holy Spirit proceeds
from the love of the Father for the Son, and through the Son
is to be poured out over the whole world, nothing is more
appropriate than that the Son in his humanity, as the head of
all creatures, should represent and effect this outpouring of
the Holy Spirit in the outpouring of his blood, and that this
latter outpouring should become the real sacrament of the
other outpouring.[20]

Here, however, Scheeben's patristic footnotes dry up, and in
cognate passages of Balthasar's *Theodramatik*, the source most
relevantly cited is the twentieth century Russian Sergei Bulgakov.
The Neapolitan Dominican Giuseppe Marco Salvati in his survey
of such Paschal Triadologies, *Teologia trinitaria della Croce*,
highlights Augustine's Sermon 52, with its affirmation that both
Father and Son were engaged on the work of the Passion, and a
homily of Origen on Ezekiel which speaks of the Father's passion
of love, but nowhere does he note any patristic reference to the
Spirit's role on Calvary.[21] It seems rather important, given the fact
that for a Catholic theory of doctrinal development "early
anticipation" (in Newman's words) is crucial, that texts witnessing
to some fuller anticipation by the Fathers of this important
extension of Trinitarian thinking should be sought. But of course
to those who would see themselves as Neo-patristic theologians –
and nothing more – that may be putting the proverbial cart well in
front of its horse. To the present writer, and continuing the quasi-
equine metaphor, it does not seem so clear that if Balaam's ass
could prophesy, the post-patristic divines of the Catholic Church
cannot furnish fresh insight into the deposit of faith also.

---

[20] M. J. Scheeben, *The Mysteries of Christianity* (Et St Louis and London 1947), pp. 446, 445.

[21] G. M. Salvati, *Teologia trinitaria della Croce* (Turin 1987), p. 98.

IV

LITTLEMORE FROM LUCERNE:
NEWMAN'S ESSAY ON DEVELOPMENT IN
BALTHASARIAN PERSPECTIVE

It is not difficult to imagine Lucerne viewed from Littlemore. The discovery of the Alps by Englishmen was a part of that Romantic Movement some of whose garments the Oxford divines stole for the better setting forth of the Gospel. Not only the miscreant Shelley and Byron but also the Wordsworths, William and Dorothy, left prose and poetry worthy of inclusion in any Alpine anthology. In 1829 Walter Scott published his "Swiss" novel, *Anne of Geierstein*. In 1835 John Ruskin made his first visit to Switzerland at the age of sixteen. Standing on the Col de la Faucille, "the spectacle opened to me the Holy Land of my future work, and my true home in this world".[1] J. M. W. Turner, Ruskin's *beau idéal* of the visual artist, had made his first visit as long ago as 1804 and would continue to travel and sketch there until 1844; his *The Lake of Thun* was perhaps his last water-colour and final canvas before his death in 1851.[2] In 1845 Dickens was at Lucerne and would return the following year to write *Dombey and Son* at Lausanne; in 1848 Matthew Arnold could be found at Thun or in the Oberland; in 1849 George Eliot was at Geneva and Elizabeth Barrett Browning at Interlaken, by now almost an English colony. In the course of the 1850s Ruskin poured out the volumes of his *Modern Painters: Their Superiority in the Art of Landscape Painting to all the Ancient Masters*; in an epilogue he would re-affirm the connection between the mountains and his aesthetic *credo*, with its central claim that

---

1 Cited in J. Wraight, *The Swiss and the British* (Wilton, Salisbury 1987), p. 227.
2 J. Gage, *J. M. W. Turner: "A Wonderful Range of Mind"* (New Haven and London 1987), p. 243.

the knowledge of what is beautiful leads on, and is the first step, to the knowledge of the things which are lovely and of good report; and [that] the laws, the life, and the joy of beauty in the material world of God are as eternal and sacred parts of his creation as, in the world of spirits, virtue; and in the world of angels, praise.[3]

By that decade, English travellers could plan their journey with the help of a variety of guide-books, from Daniel Wall's *The Traveller's Guide through Switzerland*, written as early as 1819, to John Murray's *A Handbook for Travellers in Switzerland*, published in 1838. Most visitors now wished to go higher, in plain contradiction of that pre-Romantic sensibility which made Bishop Berkeley, crossing Mont Cenis in 1714, a disagreeable companion, put "out of humour by the most horrible precipices", or John Spence in 1730 declare without a trace of irony, "I should like the Alps very much if it were not for the hills".[4] They could select among Alfred Wills' *Wanderings in the High Alps* (1856), T. W. Hinchliff's *Summer Months among the Alps* (1857), and *Peaks, Passes and Glaciers* (1859), edited by the first president of the Alpine Club, John Ball. In 1863, Thomas Cook organized his first tour to Switzerland. Entering the country at Geneva, the Cook's tourist crossed Canton Vaud to the Valais, did full justice to the Bernese Oberland, and proceeded via the Lake of Brienz to Lucerne where the ascent of the Rigi formed the climax of the trip prior to leaving Switzerland for France again via Neuchâtel.[5] The beginnings of mass tourism (the 21-day holiday cost, inclusively, £19 17s 6d) did little to deter the English literary class. In 1864 Mrs Gaskell was at Pontresina writing *Mothers and Daughters*, in 1865 Christina Rossetti almost everywhere, and in 1866 two

---

[3] J. Ruskin, *Modern Painters* (Orpington 1888), V, p. 362 (from the Epilogue to the last edition published in Ruskin's lifetime).

[4] Cited in A. Lunn, *Switzerland and the English* (London 1944), p. 42.

[5] Ruskin noted the frequency with which Turner sketched the Rigi: see I. Warrell, *Through Switzerland with Turner: Ruskin's First Selection from the Turner Bequest* (London 1995), p. 75. Newman refused to go up it: C. S. Dessain, Cong. Orat. (ed.), *John Henry Newman, Letters and Diaries* XXII (London 1972), p. 285. Cited below as *LD* XXII.

celebrated Englishmen reached Lucerne. One was Sir George Grove, the creator of the great encyclopaedia of music; the other was John Henry Newman.

It cannot be said that Newman covered himself with glory precisely as a student of Swiss scenery. Whereas in the Suisse Romande the weather had been bad, in the Oberland and at Lucerne it was, he admitted, excellent. Nonetheless, the comments in his letters on the ambient beauty of landscape are perfunctory. He reserved more space for querulousness about personal comfort – the beds at once too comfortable (the upper mattress) and not comfortable enough (the lower), the food disagreeable – too varied, though he took in his stride the serving of a seagull. Newman could no doubt have met numerous Oxford-trained clergymen: over sixty places of worship of the Church of England had been or were being built, while muscular Kingsleyan parsons were two-a-penny on the mountain ascents. Not unreasonably, he was more preoccupied with staying within the Catholic regions of a chequered eiderdown of a country: he wanted the opportunity to say or attend Mass daily. The historic significance of his Swiss journey lies in the fact that it was then, as he revealed to Aubrey de Vere in a letter of 1870, that the key notion of the *Grammar of Assent* came to him,[6] and that central notion – that certitude is itself a form of assent – he "pursued ... about the Lake of Lucerne", where hopefully things had improved since Wall had noted that "the navigation is not dangerous, provided the steersman and rowers be not intoxicated".[7] Perhaps it was as well he had not postponed his visit till after Queen Victoria's two years later, when the Lake would become quite distractingly bedizened by strings of hotels and tearooms re-named or entitled for the first time in her honour.

Knowing no German, Newman may be forgiven his failure to realize that Lucerne was the theological centre of Swiss Catholicism, and his ignorance that in 1827, when as a tutor at

---

[6] C. S. Dessain, Cong. Orat., and T. Gornall, S.J. (eds), *John Henry Newman, Letters and Diaries* XXV (Oxford 1973), p. 199.
[7] Cited in J. Wraight, *The Swiss and the British*, p. 219.

Oriel his own short-lasting theological liberalism had reached its zenith (or nadir), there had died in the lake-city one Joseph Heinrich Alois Gügler, a figure of seminal importance for the Germanophone Catholic theology of the nineteenth and twentieth centuries,[8] the star of the *Luzerner Schule* which discovered the theological possibilities of European Romanticism a generation before its equivalent at Tübingen,[9] a profound influence on Möhler whose notions of the correlative development of Church and doctrine gave Newman himself confidence that his own *Essay on Development* might not be un-Catholic, and, above all, among the principal spurs – perhaps indeed the *chief* stimulus – to the theological aesthetics of his fellow-townsman Hans Urs von Balthasar whose work constitutes among other things a superb dogmatic expansion and re-thinking of the thesis Newman put forward in tentative historical and apologetic guise in 1845.[10]

My main aim here is, then, to look at Littlemore from Lucerne, that is, to draw out of the corpus left by the most distinguished modern Swiss theologian, Balthasar, highlights that will illuminate that key work of the most distinguished English theologian of modern times, Newman.

Balthasar never singled out Newman as one of the many writers, from the Fathers to contemporary poets and dramatists, whom he honoured with a monograph or a distinct essay – all by way of exhibiting the resources of theological tradition as well as re-taking possession of those resources for his own distinctive purposes. This has obscured two important facts, and these are, first, the key role played in Balthasar's corpus at large by references to Newman and Newmanian ideas, and secondly, the way Balthasar's score provides richer dogmatic orchestration for a

---

[8] J. L. Schiffmann, *Lebensgeschichte Alois Güglers* (Augsburg 1833).

[9] For an overview, see D. Gla, *Repertorium der katholisch-theologischen Literatur in Deutschland, Oesterreich und der Schweiz*, I, 1 (Paderborn 1895).

[10] H. U. von Balthasar, *The Glory of the Lord: A Theological Aesthetics, I: Seeing the Form* (ET Edinburgh 1982), pp. 94–104. Cited below as *GL I*.

number of Newmanian themes relevant not least to the 1845 *Essay*.

Let me offer an overview of the allusions to, or expositions of Newman's ideas in the great trilogy – *Herrlichkeit*, the theological aesthetics, *Theodramatik*, the theological dramatics, and *Theologik*, the theological logic, before concentrating more especially on what Balthasar can add to a dogmatic understanding of Newman's idea of development as laid out most fully, but by no means exclusively, in that treatise of the year of his conversion to Rome.

Balthasar regarded Newman's conversion as a major example of what he termed the "Pauline" element in the total structure of ecclesial experience. Drawing on the paradigm case of the conversion of Saul of Tarsus, Balthasar proposed that an enduring factor in the construction of distinctively Christian experience in the Church lies in the phenomenon of what he called the "ever-new vertical irruption of new charisms which suddenly visit and fructify" her life.[11] The conversion to the Church, or to a more fully ecclesial life, of certain individuals outstanding in their gifts of nature and grace, can render the Church spiritually fruitful in fresh ways. For Balthasar there are no charisms – that is, no special gifts of the Spirit for the sanctification of individuals – without concomitant calls to mission, without, namely, some repercussion in a reorientation of life and consciousness in the corporate existence of the Church, at any rate in given times and places. Elsewhere, in the soon-to-be translated *Theologik*, when speaking of the Spirit and the Church as factors in theological logic, Balthasar contrasts the ecclesiastical hierarchy, whose chief gift is the discernment of spirits, with the charismatic element proper which can be moved to introduce some novelty whose legitimacy may not at first sight be obvious to the Church of office – as with the innovatory understanding of Religious life represented in the sixteenth century not only by the founder of the Society of Jesus but also by that pioneer of

---

[11] *Ibid.*, p. 354.

71

sisterhoods dedicated to teaching, better known in the German-speaking lands than in her own country, Mary Ward. Such Spirit-willed innovations come normally, Balthasar comments, either from non-ordained believers or from "priests enflamed by the Holy Ghost" – and it is in this last exalted category that Balthasar places the contribution of Newman.[12]

But in what, on Balthasar's view, scattered as this is through a medley of references in the trilogy, *did* Newman's specific contribution consist? The question can be answered by synthesizing those references. What Balthasar emphasizes about Newman is in the first place his experiential, cordial ("of the heart"), and holistic approach to the Gospel of Christ. Balthasar claims Newman as an outstanding witness for the defence in his own case for the vindication of believing experience – the ordinary spiritual experience of Christians, distinct from though intimately connected with mystical experience properly so called – as something internal to, and even decisive for, the theological enterprise. Though Balthasar is careful to construct his concept of Christian experience in such a way that it can never be *counterposed to* Church tradition or teaching whereas it can and does *amplify* both, he treats that experience nonetheless as the entrance of the believing person into those realities of which faith speaks. He sees Newman as a climactic representative of (in a term borrowed from Henri Bremond) that "metaphysics of the saints" which, emphasizing the Christian life rather than speculation, renounced the idea of relationship with God as mediated via the cosmos because its own religious sensibility was animated throughout by the desire for an immediate (if Christ-centred) contact with God.[13] Locating Newman in this way with the

---

[12] H. U. von Balthasar, *Theologik, III: Der Geist der Wahrheit* (Einsiedeln 1987), p. 292. Cited below as *TL III*.

[13] "Immediate contact": in the context of the natural knowledge of God, which is chiefly at issue in the *Grammar of Assent*, this might be thought to raise the issue of Ontologism. Balthasar cites elsewhere, relevantly, Erich Przywara's defence of Newman's illative sense: "There is no direct intuition of the primal divine Ground, even if the "conclusion" expresses itself psychologically as direct perception. This is an inchoate kind of knowledge, but in it, nonetheless, the divine is grasped as the

Rhineland mystics, Loyola and the French school culminating in his fellow-Oratorian Pierre de Bérulle, would certainly help to explain his lack of responsiveness to the Alpine glories of his 1866 travels: Newman, we might say, preserved the distinctive emotional range of early nineteenth-century Romanticism, from awe to tenderness, but displaced from its customary stimuli in the experience of physical nature.

But then, after this praise of experiential holism, when Balthasar calls such a spiritual approach the emergence of a distinctive if incomplete Christian *metaphysics* we realize that he is not praising Newman's concern with experience for any anti-intellectual bias. Linking Newman to Pascal and Kierkegaard, he describes all three as speaking not only existentially but also objectively – *sachlich* – because "they ... stood under Christ's fiery glance [the reference is surely to the opening vision of the Johannine Apocalypse] which forbade them to engage in any digressive rhetoric and simply charged them to stand firm".[14]

As Balthasar explains, with Newman the heart is the *foundation* of the intellect (as of the other particular faculties) – *not* its *rival*.[15] Where the language of the heart is used more restrictively for the affective dynamism of our subjective nature rather than our intellectual capacity to reflect what is really given in objective reality, then one would have to say that Newman's

---

Absolute, the Ground ... of all that is in the world." *Theo-drama, IV: The Action* (Et San Francisco 1994), p. 141, with reference to Przywara's *Religionsbegründung* (Freiburg 1923).

[14] *GL I*, p. 515. Balthasar characterizes this approach in general in this way: "This theology was in a new way an elevation and fulfilment of metaphysics, because explicitly and for the first time it knew how to explain *ontologically* the *ontic* (historical) event of salvation. It was historical inasmuch as it revealed to concrete man (in his condition of guilt and death) where and how transcendence is to be found. It was personal inasmuch as only *one* concrete man (and not abstract neutral human nature) could be the subject of this self-abandonment and agony, in personal love for a personal God. At the same time it was universal inasmuch as his unique self-giving and suffering opened up for all access to complete transcendence in the form of salvation." *The Glory of the Lord, V: The Realm of Metaphysics in the Modern Age* (Et Edinburgh 1991), p. 51.

[15] *GL I*, p. 167.

theology of revelation is *not* simply cordial. For him as for Augustine, the "certainty of the ultimate rightness of the 'true religion' does not rest", so Balthasar remarks, "in mere intuitions of heart and conscience or of faith, but resides in a seeing of the rightness which in the broad sense must be called an aesthetic vision and yet which stands up to rational examination and ... can even be made visible to the person who purifies his mind's eye".[16]

Newman's third kind of inspirational utility to Balthasar – after experiential holism and a vision, at once aesthetic and rational, of Christianity's "rightness" – lies in the concept, central to the *Grammar of Assent*, worked out as that was in close connection with Balthasar's native city, of the convergence of evidence as illuminated by the illative sense. Reference to this notion opens and closes the seven volumes of Balthasar's theological aesthetics, beginning with his first sketch of the idea of revelatory form, *Gestalt*, as something that itself works on our human sensibility, our apparatus of possible response, and heightens its powers, and ending with his exposition of the New Testament's wonderful fulfilment of this notion, when the Word became flesh and we saw his Glory.

In the first volume of *Herrlichkeit*, we learn how through the convergence of evidence, as traced by the illative sense, a conclusion results as something suddenly seen – which is how Balthasar's Jesuit predecessor, Pierre Rousselot, in *Les yeux de la Foi* (over against the somewhat dessicatedly rationalistic apologetics of his time), understood the relation between the rational preamble of faith and faith's apprehension of God himself, revealing.[17] But then in the last volume, a biblical theology replicates the movement of faith in its own fashion; as it works through the data of the New Testament it shows in Balthasar's words, "the 'convergence' of the lines and paths of discernment ...

---

[16] H. U. von Balthasar, *The Glory of the Lord: A Theological Aesthetics, II: Studies in Theological Styles: Clerical Styles* (Et Edinburgh 1984), p. 139. Cited below as *GL II*.
[17] *GL I*, p. 176.

on the single focal point of surpassing brightness, where the glory flares out".[18]

That glory, in Balthasar's own idiom, is the "absolute Trinitarian love of God, which discloses itself and offers itself in Jesus Christ, which disarms by its humility and simplicity every 'stronghold' of would-be mastering thought"[19] and in the substance of that claim no reader of Newman's *Parochial and Plain Sermons* is likely to drive a wedge between the Gospel preached at Littlemore and the Gospel from Lucerne. And then again in *Theodramatik*, where Balthasar is less concerned with the overall impression that Jesus made, the topic of theological aesthetics, and more with his saving action, that "centre" discerned by illation is not so much displaced as re-described when he speaks of the "ultimate lines of human destiny" as "drawn to a transcendental point of convergence" in the *Resurrection* of Christ,[20] for the Crucified and Risen One *is* the Incarnate Word, just as the One who became incarnate did so in order by sacrificial death and exaltation to show his glory. Whether we are thinking in terms of theological aesthetics or theological dramatics, or, for that matter, theological logic, it is always the case (so Balthasar thought) that theological method should "fold inwards ... towards the divine simplicity" – even though at the same time he also envisaged, significantly, a variety of theologies, grouped in two great families, the Greek and the Latin, being called to pursue that task in somewhat different ways. In an Eastern theology, each facet of the revelatory form is treated as transparent to its central epiphany, for the whole is transfigured by the divine glory. In a Western theology where doxology takes the different form of the bounden duty and service of rigorous thinking, revelation has many separate articulations in a variety of propositions and even treatises, but

---

[18] H. U. von Balthasar, *The Glory of the Lord: A Theological Aesthetics, VII: Theology: the New Covenant* (Et Edinburgh 1989), p. 18. Cited below as *GL VII*.

[19] Ibid., p. 15: "stronghold" refers to the *ochyrômata*, fortresses of worldly thought which would obstruct the knowledge of God in 2 Cor. 10.4–5.

[20] H. U. von Balthasar, *Theo-drama: Theological Dramatic Theory, II: The Dramatis Personae: Man in God* (Et San Francisco 1990), p. 94. Cited below as *TD II*.

thought, if it is to be Christian, must nonetheless lead continually along these pathways to the midpoint Jesus Christ.

This notion, which at once licenses a plurality of theologies yet provides a criterion for their evaluation, brings me to the fourth and last general lesson Balthasar learnt from Newman, and, in this case, more specifically from Newman's Tractarian background. Typical of Newman, so Balthasar thought, was a pointing to the whole truth, whilst simultaneously renouncing system.[21] Despite Newman's priesthood and later cardinalate, Balthasar, in his discussion of theological styles, places him unhesitatingly with "lay" rather than "clerical" theology. Lay theology, in Balthasar's somewhat idiosyncratic use of that phrase, means a theology which refuses to limit itself either to pastoral concerns – practical usefulness to the Church's members – or to specialization of an academic kind, and which revolts against the narrowness that often afflicts Scholastic theology, linked as the latter is to the needs of basic ecclesiastical training in seminaries or official Church schools.[22] Balthasar's principal English example is Hopkins, but, he says, he could equally well have chosen either Newman or Chesterton.[23] Newman, he stresses, while insisting that the totality of revelation is so great that it can never be encompassed in one theological system, also considered that nonetheless theology should attempt to suggest that totality. In his theological aesthetics, in the course of considering Newman's influence on Hopkins, Balthasar emphasizes the need to integrate the imagination into the structure of thinking if such evocation of the revelatory totality is to succeed – and in this connection praises the *Grammar of Assent* for doing just that, locating it in a venerable tradition of Anglican divinity with just such an aim from Coleridge to Austin Farrer and Eric Mascall.[24] In the theological dramatics, by contrast, where Balthasar is concerned less with the

---

[21] *GL II*, p. 25.

[22] *Ibid.*, p. 16.

[23] *Ibid.*, p. 21.

[24] H. U. von Balthasar, *The Glory of the Lord: A Theological Aesthetics, III: Studies in Theological Styles: Lay Styles* (Et Edinburgh 1986), pp. 353–4. Cited below as *GL III*.

response of the mind to the beauty of revelation and more with that of the will to its goodness, its saving power, he appeals again to what he takes to be the Newmanian idea that theology should evoke totality without ever claiming to englobe it – but this time in the context of the *freedom of the act of faith*. There can and should be "pointers toward the ever-greater totality" which is revelation, and yet "there must be no overwhelming proof, lest the freedom of the act of faith be over-ridden in a rationalistic way".[25]

As Balthasar remarks, "A method of proof that diminished the dramatic character of the Christ event would automatically show itself to be a failure",[26] and by this criterion, the method of the *Grammar of Assent* is a resounding success, confirming at the level of theological dramatic theory those credits which, when engaged on his project of theological aesthetics, he had already awarded it as a means, at once intellectual and aesthetic, of beginning to apprehend the divine transcendence in its embodied image, Jesus Christ.

Before leaving the general topic of Balthasar's overall indebtedness to Newman and considering more closely his attempt at a re-presentation of the themes of the 1845 *Essay* I should, however, attempt to scotch one possible misunderstanding of Balthasar's claim that Newman's theology is essentially lay in style. He in no way meant by this that Newman's distinctive thought is somehow unsuited to the use of the *Amtskirche*, that part of the Church which through ordination exercises the apostolic ministry. Indeed, if we turn to the final volume of *Theologik*, the closing work of the entire trilogy, we find Newman's clerical ideal cited as an illustration of the personal holiness which should accompany the sacramental or institutional holiness of office of the priest. The Church of office, the Petrine church, requires the Church of love, the Johannine church: thus clerical holiness is not primarily a matter of moral duty but an expression of the unity which should hold good between what Balthasar terms the objective and subjective aspects of the economy of the Holy Spirit – the Spirit in

---

[25] *TD II*, p. 130.
[26] Ibid., p. 115.

institutions, the Spirit in hearts – his Christianized version of Hegel's distinction between objective and subjective *Geist* or mind.[27]

It is time to turn to those themes which most closely mirror the motifs of the *Essay on the Development of Christian Doctrine.* Were we in this regard simply to scour Balthasar's trilogy for explicit references to the *Essay on Development,* we should be disappointed. The *Grammar of Assent,* the *University Sermons,* the "Preface" to the *Via Media, Difficulties of Anglicans,* the correspondence with the Abbé Jager, and even the reply to Peel in *The Tamworth Reading Room* figure more prominently. Surprising as it seems, given the extent of Newman's importance to Balthasar as I have charted it so far, Balthasar does not link the Oxford doctor by name with the idea of doctrinal development except in one rather cavalier reference, to be found in the extended essay on the Russian philosopher theologian Vladimir Sergeivic´ Solov'ev which forms part of the third volume of *Herrlichkeit.*[28] Let us polish off that morsel before tucking into the meat of this topic.

The association of Newman with Solov'ev would have encouraged those Anglican critics of Newman's *Essay* who considered that, despite his early strictures on Pusey's Germanophilia, he had sold out at the last to the evolutionary and organicist pretensions of German Idealism, so that the *Essay* led not so much to Rome as via Rome to Berlin and infidelity. Basing himself on Solov'ev's *Istoriya i budushchnost' teokratii* ("The History and Future of Theocracy"), written between 1885 and 1887 and, though not completed, published as a substantial fragment at Zagreb for fear of adverse reaction from the Tsarist censors, Balthasar identifies the central notion of Solov'ev's thought as process – a notion grounded in the intuition at the heart of German Idealism, but confirmed by the Russian thinker's research into cosmology, cultural history and the "evolution of Christological truth in the dogmatic development of the Church –

---

[27] *TL III,* p. 322.

[28] *GL III,* p. 283.

sketched by Solov'ev almost more painstakingly than by Newman". Solov'ev inferred, in Balthasar's summary, a "progressive eschatological embodiment of the Divine Idea in worldly reality", and while the word "Idea" here may remind us of a key term of the *Essay on Development*, the general conceptual idiom is evidently far removed from Newman's, putting us more in mind, perhaps, of what Chesterton called

> fantastic professors in fiction, who wave their hands and say, "Thus do we mount to the ineffable heights of pure and radiant Being"; or, worse still, of actual professors in real life, who say, "All Being is Becoming; and is but the evolution of Not-Being by the law of its Being"[29]

– a reference to the Neo-Hegelianism fashionable in Chesterton's early manhood, not least at Oxford. I must not, however, be unfair to Solov'ev, whose treatise, with its account of the delicate equilibrium of the mutually defining offices of king, prophet and priest in a Christian society, is more than a little reminiscent, at any rate in its formal structure, of the "Preface" to the *Via Media*.[30] But a Balthasarian re-statement of the themes of the 1845 *Essay* does not lie in this direction.

To arrive at that re-statement by counting references to Newman will not serve, for it lies in the integration, conscious or unconscious, of Newmanian motifs in the deep structure of Balthasar's theological thought. There are three of these, and they resolve ultimately into claims about, respectively, Jesus, Mary and Peter.

The single most important contribution of Balthasar's work to a theological understanding of the *Essay* concerns the notion of objective revelatory form, central as that is to the theological aesthetics, which aesthetics are themselves, on Balthasar's own account, the necessary prolegomena to theological dramatics, for

---

[29] G. K. Chesterton, *St Thomas Aquinas* (London 1933), pp. 180–1.

[30] See for instance the exposition of the "inter-dependent nature of their functions and authority" in J. Sutton, *The Religious Philosophy of Vladimir Solovyov: Towards a Reassessment* (London 1988), p. 86.

we must grasp the Word of God in human guise if we are to respond to the action which it undertakes on the world-stage – the whole finding its culmination in the theological logic which considers what truth must be if the divine beauty and its saving goodness are really given us through the historic revelation, *really* given us, or as we say in conversational English, given us really *and truly*. The notion of the objective form of revelation, in other words, plays the same pivotal role in Balthasar's theological vision as does that of the Christian "Idea" in Newman's *Essay*. But more than that: the two notions are not just similarly important; they are also similar *tout court*. Or to put it more provocatively, it was to this concept of the objective revelatory form of the Gospel that Newman's mind and sensibility reached out, without ever quite giving it adequate articulation. The "objective existence" of Christianity, its "historically unmistakable and bold outlines", history's "imprinting on our minds" Christianity's "living image": once the student of Newman has read the opening volume of Balthasar's *Herrlichkeit – Schau der Gestalt, Seeing the Form*, these phrases taken from Newman's own "Introduction" to his *Essay* will never, I venture to predict, be separable henceforth from that key idea of theological aesthetics.[31] And how could we miss, after immersion in Balthasar, the aesthetic model underlying this crucial statement in the *Essay*'s opening chapter "On the Development of Ideas":

> Ideas are not ordinarily brought home to the mind, except through the medium of a variety of aspects; like bodily substances, which are not seen except under the clothing of their properties and influences, and can be walked round and surveyed on opposite sides and in different perspectives and in contrary lights. And as views of a material object may be taken from points so remote or so distinct that they seem at first sight incompatible, and especially as their shadows will be disproportionate or even monstrous, and yet all these will be harmonised together by taking account of the point of vision or the surface of projection, so also all the representations of

---

[31] J. H. Newman, *An Essay on the Development of Christian Doctrine: The Essay of 1845* (Harmondsworth 1973), pp. 69, 72, 74. Cited below as *ED*.

> an idea, even all the misrepresentations, are capable of mutual reconciliation and adjustment, and of a resolution into the subject to which they belong, and their contrariety, when explained, is an argument for its substantiveness and integrity, and their variety for its originality and power.[32]

Or as Balthasar puts it, "the unity of the form offers a fullness of approaches, doors and possibilities for entry".[33] In those words from the concluding volume of *The Glory of the Lord*, Balthasar applies to the biblical revelation with its centre in Christ, as to a surpassingly pre-eminent case, what in the opening volume of *Theologik*, in a description of the truth of reality at large, he has said of *any* significant form. The human mind draws from the imaged world around us *eine Ganzheit der Gestalt*, a "wholeness of form", whereby our shifting perceptions of things come to appear as so many presentations, from different angles, of the same reality.[34] The greater the intrinsic significance of the form – in Newman's vocabulary, the *idea* – the more varied the perspectives it provokes and offers to our gaze.

Where Balthasar's account *adds* to what Newman left us is his insistence that, however many *aspects* the idea may manifest, however many "perspects" – *perspectives* – it may permit, it retains a unity which transcends all of them thanks to its possession of an organizing centre. And this midpoint of the form is *Jesus Christ himself.* In his capacity to enable the intersection of a multitude of relationships, vertical and horizontal, to past and to future, he constitutes himself, in his life, death and Resurrection, the indispensable reference point of all theology and all contemplation worthy of the Christian name. A putative doctrinal development, therefore, will be able to establish its claim, if and only if it can show that it forms a connection in the total nexus of relations of which Christ is the centre – whether or not this was explicitly recognized by the witnesses of the apostolic generation themselves. Such a Christological re-casting of Newman's "divine Idea" has the

---

[32] *Ibid.*, p. 95.
[33] *GL* VII, p. 15.
[34] H. U. von Balthasar, *Theologik, I: Wahrheit der Welt* (Einsiedeln 1985), p. 147.

merit among others of aligning Newman's account more fully with what is now the most authoritative statement of the Catholic communion on this subject – the Dogmatic Constitution *Dei Verbum*, on Divine Revelation, of the Second Vatican Council, where speaking precisely of the "inner unity" of the "plan of revelation", Christ is declared to be simultaneously revelation's Mediator *and its fullness*.[35] I have showed elsewhere that this text was almost certainly indebted to the Christocentric view of doctrinal development worked out by Balthasar's colleague and friend Henri de Lubac, who sought to inject into the narrower topic of the development of doctrine a shot of that Christ-centredness which, in the steps of Barth, Balthasar tried to revive in the Catholic theology of revelation as a whole.[36] It is by coming to see some facet of the revelatory form in its relation to that form's midpoint that one comes to register what Newman calls in the *Essay* its "due shape and complete proportions".[37]

I come now to the second principal motif relevant to the *Essay on Development,* and that concerns the mode in which such theologically aesthetic perception of shape and proportion, in Newman's words, "spreads through a community and attains general reception".[38] A major harbinger of the *Essay* had been the 1843 Sermon on "The Theory of Developments in Religious Doctrine" where Newman had put forward as an archetype of the Church developing doctrine the Blessed Virgin Mary, as she appears in the Lucan infancy Gospel, ruminating, turning over in her mind, the impression left by the childhood of Christ. *Dei Verbum*, once again, takes up this Marian perspective in its own brief theology of development when it ascribes "growth in the understanding of the realities and the words ... handed down" (in Tradition) to, in the first place, the "contemplation and study made by believers, who treasure these things in their hearts and

---

[35] *Dei Verbum* 2.

[36] A. Nichols, O.P., *From Newman to Congar: The Idea of Doctrinal Development from the Victorians to the Second Vatican Council* (Edinburgh 1990), pp. 195–213.

[37] *ED*, p. 109.

[38] Ibid.

through the intimate understanding of spiritual things they experience".[39] What Balthasar provides is a fuller dogmatic understanding of why all development of doctrine can usefully be regarded as issuing from this Marian matrix.

For Balthasar, Mary's faith-response to the incarnating Word constitutes a kind of *a priori* structure – to use the language of Kantian epistemology – governing the corporate faith of the entire subsequent Church. It is, to his mind, a presupposition of the Incarnation that there should be, within the purely human realm, a receiving subject to whom the final revelation could be made in more than simply an approximative way. As he writes:

> Somewhere, in the name of all mankind, a *fiat* with no internal boundaries must exist in response to the final Word of God that continually transcends all understanding, a *fiat* that goes all the way to the end with God's Word in unreserved agreement, in the meditative attempt to understand [and at this point Balthasar involves the same Lucan texts indicated by Newman in the sermon of 1843]; ... and this [so Balthasar continues, with reference now to the development of doctrine in the Church of Christ born from Mary's faith] *sets in motion an endless historical process.*[40]

Thanks to the "Marian principle", as Balthasar terms it, the entire later Church lives from this Marian matrix. As the God-bearer who is such precisely through her faith, Mary "encloses all Christians within herself and brings them forth from herself along with their experience of faith".[41] As Mary's "archetypal" experience passes over into the "imitative" experience of the Church's members, the privileges of personal intimacy with Christ as a result of which she enjoyed the tact which enabled her to judge rightly of her Son, centre-point of revelation as he is, are gradually expropriated (in Balthasar's key term) in favour of ordinary believers. And this, for Balthasar, explains the prophetical office of the Church, or more precisely the prophetical tradition to which Newman contrasted – though in no contestational spirit – the

---

[39] *Dei Verbum* 8.
[40] *GL VII*, p. 94. Italics added.
[41] *GL I*, p. 340.

episcopal tradition in the 1837 treatise on that subject. To Balthasar that contrast is not so much a revindication of the rights of the Christian laity as a way of speaking about the dramatic interplay between the mystical Church, the *ecclesia Mariana*, and the Church of office, the Church of Peter.[42]

And that way of speaking – with Newman, with Balthasar – of the inter-relation of the *sensus Ecclesiae* and the magisterium brings me in conclusion to the third motif of the idea of development re-worked in Swiss perspective, and that concerns the Petrine teaching-office which, in the manner of the early Cyprian, Balthasar ascribes to the entire Catholic episcopate – while reserving, of course, a quite special place for the Roman church and bishop in this regard. In the *Essay on Development* Newman wrote, "If Christianity is both social and dogmatic, and intended for all ages, it must, humanly speaking, have an infallible expounder."[43]

From the late 1850s to the late 1870s Newman would be preoccupied by the need to do justice to the role of the laity on the one hand and that of the Roman pontiff on the other in the expository process. In the Marian church, the living faith of the believer, remarks Balthasar, echoing Newman, has regard to

> a totality of fulness which the believer can discern through the Holy Spirit, at least to the extent that, while he can never attain an overview of it, he can detect every substantial omission from it as a violation of the law of the whole, of inner proportion, or, rather, of the law of God's self-giving, which is "always more".[44]

The *magisterium externum* of episcopal tradition in the church of Peter exists to serve the holism of this instinct of faith in the *magisterium internum* of prophetic tradition in the church of Mary.[45] Like a seismographic instrument (Balthasar's simile), the

---

[42] H. U. von Balthasar, *Theo-drama, III: The Dramatis Personae: The Person in Christ* (Et San Francisco 1992), p. 358.

[43] *ED*, p. 177.

[44] *TD II*, pp. 99–100.

[45] *TL III*, p. 302.

teaching office will react when some "substantial underground tremor threatens the totality or catholicity of revelation".[46] The task of that office is to re-create the inner harmony of the Gospel's organic unity when through some distorting unilateralism of emphasis it gets upset. Balthasar accurately reflects Newman's concern in the "Preface" to the *Via Media* that the pope and his curia should not attempt to replace the function of the theologian in the schools. Yet his explanation of their inter-relation, I venture to say, improves on Newman's, in stressing that "the teaching-office is not primarily concerned with the formulation but with the charge it bears [for "the same proposition can bear a different charge in the mouth of Augustine and in that of Jansen"]. Its particular definitions and condemnations are always made with a view to re-establishing the endangered totality."[47] Balthasar preserves the pastoral finality of magisterial inventions which led Newman to attribute those interventions to the regal office of the Church, but at the same time does not separate them from the teaching office – the prophetic office of the Church in its specifically episcopal form, which we must surely regard as the inconvenience, the implausibility indeed, of Newman's version.

Newman wrote to his brother Francis, "I have been sent into Switzerland to be made young again".[48] Another master of singing school would follow him to finish a lament for the decrepitude not of an individual but of Christendom's civilization. But if Eliot, finishing *The Waste Land* at Lausanne in 1922, could end nonetheless on a note of hope, in the Sanskrit invocation of a peace that passes all understanding, how much the more, for those whose life is theologically grounded, can there be hope of rejuvenescence for that Church and faith which Newman embraced at such cost in 1845. Balthasar's theological achievement, with its confidence that the Gospel can salve the wounds, untangle the contradictions, and lift the limitations, of contemporary culture shows us that Pentecostal grace has not lost

---

[46] *Ibid.*, p. 101.
[47] Ibid.
[48] *LD* XXII, p. 299.

its freshness in our time. Not the least aspect of that *recursus ad fontes* lies in Balthasar's encouragement that we should look at Newman with the originality as well as fidelity Newman himself brought to the faith of the Church. An "idea" may "develop", showing new sides of itself, if only we view Littlemore from Lucerne.

V

BALTHASAR'S AIMS IN HIS *THEOLOGICAL AESTHETICS*

The sheer bulk of Hans Urs von Balthasar's *The Glory of the Lord*;[1] the variety of sources – both theological and philosophical – on which it draws and the diversity in time of their origin – Hellenic, Hellenistic, Roman, biblical, patristic, medieval, early modern and modern; the lack of any clear argumentative development in the six volumes (seven in English) as a whole; the abundance of Balthasar's illustrative material and his seeming inability to stop himself from running after hares he has started (a difficulty compounded, no doubt, by the circumstance of owning his own publishing house and so encountering no externally enforced limits either of length or of expense): all these factors help to explain the discouragement of readers when faced with the Herculean labour of actually reading this monumental work. There is, accordingly, a problem in "Balthasar reception": the message of *Herrlichkeit* as a whole is not getting through. In this article I propose to fill this gap by asking, What did Balthasar intend to achieve in writing this work?

What, in other words, are the aims of the theological aesthetics, supposing – as is surely natural – that we treat the text as evidence for those aims? Artists may sometimes surprise themselves by their work, and we can perhaps regard Balthasar as a theological artist who is trying to extend the Christian vision of the world by a creative manipulation of traditional ideas, sources and themes. But on the whole we regard the artefacts artists leave behind – on canvas or in print – as evidential for our reading of their intentions – though, naturally, conflicting interpretations of

---

[1] *The Glory of the Lord: A Theological Aesthetics*, 7 Vols. (Edinburgh 1982-1989) Et of *Herrlichkeit: Eine theologische Ästhetik*, 6 Vols. (Einsiedeln 1961-1969). Henceforth I refer to this work as *Herrlichkeit*, though I cite the volume numbers of the Et throughout.

such intentions can arise, in which case appeal may be made to anything they may have said autobiographically about what they were doing.

Nothing I shall say about the aims of *Herrlichkeit* will be gainsaid by Balthasar's own, very brief, account of what he was about, as that is found in, above all, four short overviews of his theological production written under the titles "Reckoning" (*Rechenschaft*), in 1965; "A Decade On" (*Noch ein Jahrzehnt*), in 1975; "Epilogue" (*Epilog*), in 1987, and finally, in 1988, "A Retrospective" (*Rückblick*), published in the year of the newly nominated cardinal's death.[2]

Balthasar's first aim, in the early sections of the first volume of *Herrlichkeit* is to show us why we need such a thing as a "theological aesthetics" at all. Why should we want to invite such a creature into the house of theological culture in the first place? For his part, Balthasar wants to make us aware what a strange question this is: what has happened to us, as human beings first of all, and then as Christians, that we do not see it as something sublimely obvious that the biblical revelation – like, it should be added, everything else – is somehow related to beauty?

There was a time, Balthasar proposes, when everything that was real, everything that stood up to the measure of truth – all that is *ens* and *verum*, as the Scholastics would say – was experienced as in some fashion beautiful. And to go back long before those terms – being, truth, beauty – and their interrelations were formulated by the Christian thought of the Western Middle Ages, to return, in fact, to the fountain-head of the Western experience of humanity in ancient Hellas, the Greeks seem to have encountered the world as a world transfigured by a god-like radiance which touched events, people and things: at least Balthasar believes so, in line with a long German tradition of reverential interpreters of the Greek experience, from the poet Hölderlin at the end of the eighteenth century to the philosopher Heidegger in the middle of

---

[2] See, respectively, *Mein Werk: Durchblicke* (Einsiedeln-Freiburg 1990), pp. 62-9; 76-7; *Epilog* (Einsiedeln-Trier 1987), pp. 45-52; and (once again) *Mein Werk*, p. 94.

the twentieth. What a contrast with the typically modern experience of reality which is, so Balthasar says – taking, we may think, a somewhat jaundiced view – essentially one of a world where all is brute facticity until meanings are projected on it by ourselves. Certainly the Greeks ran together the concepts of the good and the beautiful: the two formed a differentiated unity, the unity of *kalokagathia*. When the good ceases to be related to the beautiful, Balthasar points out, goodness loses its self-evidence. In other words, people start asking, Why be good, why follow the good, why admire the good? Just to say that a life is good, or that some piece of acting exemplifies a virtue, is no longer (for moderns like ourselves) to draw forth the response, So it must be wonderful! For that earlier sensibility, through recognizing beautiful goodness, people were at once aware of the love-worthiness of something – it could be the pattern of a life, or some natural non-human reality, or an artefact like the vase apostrophized by John Keats in his *Ode on a Grecian Urn*. In each case people were struck by the radiance which shone out through some form. And this, explains Balthasar, would always have been pertinent to truth, to the real intelligibility of things, for that real intelligibility is always in some way incarnate, even if it be only in the sounds of language. At all levels of reality we have to do with spirit expressing itself through form, and of this earthly beauty is the paradigm.

Clearly enough, all this is philosophically important. But Balthasar wants us, by means of it, to take hold of something else. What he is really driving at in this lament over the loss of beauty from the world at large is something specifically evangelical, to do with the gospel of Jesus Christ. Our capacity to perceive what Balthasar calls "the primordial phenomenon of the beautiful", is a necessary condition for our being evangelized, for receiving the gospel. Becoming, remaining and growing as a Christian depends on our enjoying access to the wondrous beauty of a unique form, Jesus Christ, as given us by the God who is the primal Creator of images and remains so in his communication with us in revelation. The re-Christianization of Western civilization depends on a few people at least (at any rate to begin with) getting this message.

Thus although Balthasar speaks of form in connection with the forms of nature, and such human life-forms as marriage (which he considers, incidentally, a very instructive case since it suggests how biology conditions but does not explain form, and how the materials a scientist might investigate can be animated, therefore, by a form that in itself is not material), and though he also – and this comes closer to his central concern – looks at how the saints are key forms for the Catholic Christian precisely because the image of their lives is engagingly loveable, nevertheless, his real focus is Jesus Christ himself, whom he wants to present as summing up the entire many-sided yet ultimately unitary form of God's self-revelation in salvation history. Everything in the Old Testament leads up in one way or another to this form, just as everything in the New Testament Church issues out of it.

So in this Christ-centred but by no means exclusively biblical fashion, Balthasar would recover for us – as a theologian – the "lost transcendental" of beauty – alongside *ens* and *verum*, *pulchrum* – and more especially beauty's biblical correlate (one can hardly just say "biblical equivalent"), glory. And by this means Balthasar aims at nothing less than the wholesale transformation of Catholic theology in its two main branches. And what are those two branches? They are, firstly, fundamental theology – which says what revelation is and how we come to find it credible; and secondly, dogmatic theology – which explores revelation's content, the various truths about the triune God, Christ, salvation, the Church, human destiny and that of the cosmos: truths which revelation puts forward.

Now Balthasar is aware that this is going to strike people as a somewhat unusual project. After all, asking why do you accept the Christian faith and what is it that, by that faith, you believe in, is not normally met by getting the answers: I believe because faith is beautiful, and what I believe in is the beauty of God. Such replies might well sound self-indulgent and mawkish, or superficial and dilettantish. So Balthasar now has to show that working out a theological aesthetics is not an unprecedented enterprise for a Christian thinker. What, I think, he really aims to do here is to meet the objections he expects from serious-minded Protestants. Because of their strong insistence – an insistence Balthasar in fact echoes – that revelation is something different and unconditionally new, something that stems from beyond culture, beyond society (i.e. it is not just human reactions to the world dressed up as something special but really the very word of God in human guise), such people might well feel that all this beauty stuff, with glory being the biblical version of the beauty that is found in nature, people, art, is simply too tangential to the scriptural revelation to be a suitable perspective in which to view its contents. Actually, Balthasar cannot show the contrary until he has finished *Herrlichkeit*. But at least he can demonstrate awareness of the problem.

He agrees that once we begin thinking in aesthetic terms we have a tendency to glorify the world, not God. Taking stock of the way things satisfy the aesthetic judgement of human beings and so delight their faculties can lead the world to pride itself on its loveliness, such that the object of marvelling – of what both Aristotle and the Gospels call *thaumazein*, being lost in wonder at something – is displaced from God to the world of nature humanly transformed, a world (in great part) of cultural artefacts, and thus an extension of ourselves. That way lies idolatry. But, Balthasar asks, if that displacement happens, cannot revelation, with theology at its service, point this out? And in any case, divine judgement on the world as the work of humankind does not always mean condemnation of the world: to think so would be the narrowest, most mean-minded kind of Protestantism. Divine judgement can also mean the assumption of what is human into the new life of grace, as when Jesus told a scribe who questioned him, You (thought you have not yet come to faith in me and my message) are not far from the Kingdom. It would be wrong just to presume that the role of grace is always to snap whatever links there may seem to be between natural beauty and supernatural glory. And appealing to a celebrated term in Catholic philosophy and theology, could there not be analogy – neither complete identity nor total dissimilarity – between the beautiful in creation and the glorious in the re-creation or new creation? Could there not be, in this respect as in others, analogy between the natural world and the world of God? Does not theology have to admit that the values in the world around us can and should be ascribed in a pre-eminent way to their ultimate Source, God? Can theology deny that the redemption and final consummation or transfiguration of the world must reflect, and at the very least equal, the artistry with which God made the world in the first place? Can it eliminate from the Resurrection faith of the first Christians the conviction that the very glory of God, exceeding all natural beauty, was manifested on this earth through the form of Christ's risen flesh?

Such biblical writers as, in the Old Testament, the authors of Ecclesiasticus and Wisdom, and, in the New, Paul and John, can surely be described as setting out contemplatively to explore the marvel of the saving work of God in, respectively, Israel and Jesus Christ. And that is the cue for Balthasar to move on to the offensive, and propose that all theology that neglects what is beautiful in revelation will finish in a dead end, incapable of permanently inspiring anybody, or fructifying anything in an abiding way. All the great theologies of the Church have been in some sense beautiful creations, something Balthasar will try to convince us of by judicious selection in the second and third volumes of *Herrlichkeit*.

None of this is to say, however, that marrying talk of the beautiful to revelation is easy or straightforward. The historical materials in volume one of *Herrlichkeit* are designed to show us some of the pitfalls that can occur. Only in volumes six and seven, the concluding biblical volumes, shall we see how Balthasar thinks this marriage should be celebrated, though a number of important hints are dropped in the metaphysical volumes, four and five, where he describes how the glory of being – the wonderfulness of reality in its global meaning – has been perceived by pagans, Christians and post-Christians, and so gives us a feel for specifically evangelical beauty, for the difference in these matters which the biblical revelation makes.

But meanwhile I must explain what Balthasar is aiming at in the remainder of his prolegomena to *Herrlichkeit*, after calming, to his own satisfaction at least, the fears of those who consider the aesthetic to be opposed to the moral and so, a fortiori, to the religious. In saying that the revelation given in Christ is credible because it is in a unsurpassable fashion worthy of our love, and sweeps us off our feet by its beauty, Balthasar aims to bring together fundamental theology or apologetics and dogmatic theology or doctrine, and moreover to bring them together in the closest union that the teaching of the Catholic Church will allow.

In standard manuals of apologetics in Balthasar's young manhood and middle age, fundamental theology was based on rational argument for the existence of God, and for the idea that human beings could receive a communication from the side of God were one offered them, along with historical arguments that such a communication had actually happened in Jesus, as proved by the signs which attended his life (miracles, the fulfilment of prophecy, his moral perfection). The gap between such argumentation and actually believing in biblical revelation was then closed by appeal to something happening deep within us, when interior grace begins to illuminate our minds and attract our wills so that, by means of the arguments and evidences, we are brought to something greater than any rational or inferred conclusion – namely, to faith in Christ. In this way the "standard" believer comes to accept as truth the teaching, about the Trinity, the identity and saving purpose of Jesus Christ, and so forth, which Christ, his apostles and the Church he founded propose to us: doctrinal truths, then, in themselves quite separate from the grounds we have for believing them via apologetics.

Balthasar, by contrast, wants to make our initial perception of the beauty of doctrine – of the picture Jesus paints of the triune God in his saving design, not only in words but in gestures – the main factor in our conversion to belief in Christ in the first place. Getting a first glimpse of the form of Christ begins a process of enlightenment which adapts our powers to God's self-revelation, such that when we set all this down on paper it turns out that apologetics is really incipient dogmatics, and dogmatics is just matured apologetics.

Now I said that Balthasar wants to recast the relation of fundamental and dogmatic theology, the study of how we find revelation credible and what it is we actually find ourselves believing when we do so, by turning that interrelation into the tightest union compatible with the official teaching of Catholicism. That qualification is important. Imagine what would have happened had Balthasar identified apologetics and dogmatics *tout court*. He would have ended up with some kind of fideism. Such fideism could be of a Protestant kind, where, as in Reformation dogmatics, nature and rationality are regarded as so corrupted by the Fall that they provide us with no ground to stand on in assessing the claims of revelation, or where, as in the twentieth-century Protestant neo-Orthodoxy of Karl Barth, a more subtle case can be propounded to the effect that nature and rationality – all beings and all our powers of reflection on being – are from the outset Christocentrically ordered by God, destined (namely) to find their consistency, stability and integrity in Jesus Christ, the Word Incarnate, and in him alone, with the result, once again, that there is nowhere outside dogmatics which will support us in reviewing revelation's claim.

Alternatively, such fideism could be of what is increasingly called a post-modernist kind, where the history of metaphysics and the attempt to find a foundation for our rational procedures are said now to have collapsed, thus opening a way – according to the Christian-theological version of post-modernism – for the doctrines of Christ and, especially, the Holy Trinity to triumph as the only available justification for such themes as the need to respect others in their otherness and particularity on which, so it is said, the universalizing claims of metaphysics and philosophical rationality have foundered. But Balthasar is not a fideist; he leaves a place for reason vis-à-vis faith, for nature vis-à-vis grace, for the common being studied by metaphysicians vis-à-vis the gift of new being which is grace (the first volume of his trilogy, *Theologik I*, shows as much), though for reasons internal to his project in the theological aesthetics he downplays rather than accentuates these distinctions in this context.

For Balthasar aims to show that the light which illlumines us in faith does not just break forth in our minds in a purely subjective way, even though this be a change in our subjectivity caused by God himself. More importantly, this "light" breaks forth from within the revelatory form which is Jesus Christ, as we begin to encounter this form, and see it as making an impact on us, beautifully ordered whole of saving goodness as it is, and ultimately as stunning us, since in the final analysis it is nothing less than God's own self-revelation. The power of this Christ-form, what the Church's faith, in keeping with the Scriptures, calls the Holy Spirit, can catch up that desire for transcendence, that desire to be and to be with something more than we are which is inscribed in our nature (as Pascal remarks, only what transcends us can satisfy us) and turn this needy desiring of ours into a mighty drive which carries us towards the reality of God now thrown open to us in Christ Jesus. In other words, the subjective evidence for revelation is, at its highest, the way this form, Jesus Christ, is compellingly radiant – and all other features like the role of miracles, prophecy, and the moral perfection of Jesus as a self-proclaimed envoy of God, must find their bearings within that context and that alone.

What we are dealing with in theological aesthetics is the study of how we come, enraptured, to see God, the world and ourselves in relation to God and the world with new eyes, thanks to our perception of the form of God's self-disclosure. It is because Balthasar aims to show us that the Christ-form in all its objective novelty and originality has the power to change our understanding of the world and our habitual sensibility in this way that he adopts a reserved attitude towards the historical-critical method as applied to the Jesus of the Gospels – with its necessarily somewhat reduced and minimal conclusions about the Jesus of history, and argues instead that the real Jesus is found only by looking through the lens of the New Testament canon as a whole, guided in so doing by the liturgy and teaching of the Church born from his Spirit.

In volumes two and three of *Herrlichkeit* Balthasar reassures us that we are not the first to tread this path. All twelve of the figures he exhibits to us in those volumes, from Irenaeus of Lyons in the second century to Charles Péguy in the twentieth, have passed this way before. The purpose of Balthasar's twelve "studies in theological style" is to show how rich are the ways the "glory of the Lord", delineated abstractly in the opening volume of *Herrlichkeit*, has been beheld and described. Two criteria were at work, he tells us, in his choice of "stars" with which to stud the sky of his theological world: intrinsic excellence and historical efficacy. In the first place these will be: "a series of Christian theologies and world-pictures of the highest rank"; but secondly, they will not be supernovae exploding unobserved so much as the theologies which "have illuminated and shaped Christian culture through the centuries".[3] In point of fact, Balthasar claims that these criteria coincide: in this domain there can be no real efficacy without true excellence. He does not aim to bring these twelve theologies into any sort of systematic unity by treating them as building-blocks for a synthesis larger than themselves. But he does expect us to grasp their harmonies, the way they echo, or at least fit in with each other, like instruments complementing one another in an orchestral score. That metaphor of the symphony of theologies is actually his own, for he takes their harmony to prove that (in his words) they "all play from the same score which both transcends and embraces them".

Balthasar does not conceal the fact that the centres of interest of these writers – five "clerical stylists", i.e., Church doctors working in Greek and Latin, from Irenaeus to Bonaventure, and seven "lay" ones, i.e., vernacular writers, from Dante to Péguy – are very different. But this is not, he says, a problem. It is perfectly natural that one theology will centre its

---

[3] *The Glory of the Lord, II: Studies in Theological Style: Clerical Style* (Et Edinburgh 1984), p. 13.

sense of glory on God himself (so that all else is lovely only in so far as God shines forth in it) and another on his revelation in its mediating role in this regard (so that beauty belongs primarily to God's self-displayal in creation and salvation), and a third on Jesus Christ as, in his two natures, "the synthesis of God and the world" (here, where redemption in the Son takes centre stage, it is the beauty of suffering love which, above all, strikes and overwhelms the observer), or yet again, on the Spirit of Christ, poured out on humankind from Father and Son as the gift of a share in their glory whereupon the focus shifts to the theme of transfiguration.

This plurality of centres of interest, which can co-exist happily as so many perspectives in mutual collusion, is mirrored, Balthasar goes on to explain, in the variety of styles in which these theologies, with their distinct foci, come to expression. Here too he feels no need to retract his claim that a correspondence exists between the glory of revelation and its imitative expression in theological beauty. The divine freedom, in its choice of vehicle in the history of the Church's tradition, is not likely to be less free than its human counterpart, and we know it is typical of human artistic expression that the beauty an artist creates comes about in freedom: great art conveys at one and the same time the impression of disciplined necessity (no detail, we feel, can be other than it is) and yet sovereign freedom (the whole need not have been at all). So why not accept that the living revelation of God is not just possessed of form, but can actually create form – that revelation can call forth in history a vast array of great theologies whose inner form it inspires.

It is these "inner forms" (rather than the outward stylistic qualities which are their sacrament) that Balthasar will try to capture in these dozen monographs that follow, on finishing which we can, I think, fairly allow him to have made his point, wander off though he may and does. The cumulative effect of substantial essays on writers from Anselm to Pascal, from Dante to Hopkins, is to persuade the reader that there have indeed been many and varied practitioners of theological aesthetics in the Church.

Not by chance, however, does Balthasar end with the French poet, social critic and lay theologian Péguy: volumes two and three reach their climax in this figure. In Péguy's theological aesthetic better than anywhere else (better even than in the Fathers, of whose work he finds Péguy's to be the extension), Balthasar locates elements he will take up in the final volumes of *Herrlichkeit* on Old and New Covenants when he will speak in his own voice. First, like Péguy, he will give a key role to the experience of Israel. Secondly, following Péguy, he will take the relationship of Old and New Covenants as decisive for aesthetics, for here the dialogue between God and Israelite man in the covenant, the Law, the prophetic word and the cultus gives way to a divine "self-showing" (*Sich-zeigen*), "self-speaking" (*Sich-sagen*), "self-giving", (*Sich-geben*) in human bodily form. And so, thirdly, with Péguy he will treat the transcendence of Christ's Godhead as emerging from the visibility of his human figure. Certainly, Balthasar wants us to drink from the ancient springs of patristic thought and of the medievals who were the continuators of the Fathers. Not for nothing is he a representative of the movement of patristic *ressourcement* in the mid-twentieth-century Church. Certainly, too, he wants us to take seriously the theological contribution made by poets, novelists and dramatists. Not for nothing, again, was he the translator of Claudel's odes, the commentator on Bernanos's novels, the interpreter of Reinhold Schneider's theatre – and got his fingers rapped by more high-and-dry Scholastic theologians for treating the works of these writers as authentic lay theology, authoritative voices of Christian experience under grace. But above all Balthasar is, like Barth, a biblical theologian, for whom Scripture is the supreme source, the true soul of theology.

So why in volume four does Balthasar turn to look at the "metaphysics of antiquity"? If not just to make a display of his classical learning where the mythology, philosophy and religious thought of the ancient world are concerned, what purpose does this serve? The answer is that it illustrates the element of theological aesthetics that is drawn from general religious metaphysics, from the sensibility and thinking of humankind at large. And this is important not only because it constitutes a preamble of faith, a preparation for the gospel, a demonstration of how there are features of being at large and humanity at large which alert us to the theological aesthetics the gospel will commend. Appealing to the pagans is even more important for enabling Balthasar to show how to grasp revelation is to grasp revelation's going beyond all the mind of man has conceived, all the heart of man imagined.

On the one hand, the Church needs all the help she can get in the task of refreshing our sense of the splendour of being, helpful preparation for our grasp of biblical glory as this is, and she has never been averse to drawing such help from pagan sources. On the other hand, and more primordially, the appeal to the classics is a sign not of weakness but of strength. Balthasar does not turn to Greece and Rome – which stand here for all experience outside the biblical covenant – owing to a fear that the revelation to Israel and, in Christ, to the Church will prove to be really rather parochial. On the contrary, so vast is the sweep of that revelation that it requires theologians to seek out that other immensity to which it is addressed – what Balthasar calls *Geist*: the human spirit open of its nature as it is to the being of all that exists. And what Balthasar tries to show is that, in inadequate yet cumulatively impressive ways, the mythology, philosophy and religion of the ancient world point to the fundamentally divine nature of beauty, beauty's quality as an epiphany of the divine – the divine not simply as inserted into the world from above but as welling up from below, from the wellspring of creation. Accordingly, the Church's earliest thinkers felt no need to disengage a purely revelational view of beauty from the philosophical. They found that, in an integrated account of being, the beauty of the world and God's better beauty, grace, do not compete but collaborate.

What Balthasar would like us to see is the way the Church consolidated an all-embracing aesthetic inherited from antiquity – first from a period dominated by myth, where the human being encounters *tò on*, "what is", in, above all, the form of dramatic images, then secondly, from a succeeding age where wisdom predominates as the nascent discipline of philosophy begins to produce instead concepts of reality, prior to entering, thirdly, an epoch of renewed religiosity (with Virgil in the West, Plotinus in the East) when concepts are relativized through a pointing to mystery. And all that is valuable in all of that, says Balthasar, was captured by the Church's single greatest divine, St Thomas Aquinas, when he presented the beauty of finite dependent being as reflecting the glory of the infinite subsistent being from whom it receives everything it has. It is the Thomas who knows how infinitely the divine Essence transcends common being yet for whom that common being is no commonplace thing but something irradiated by glory, and who grasps, moreover, that revelation does not nullify a natural theology but raises and completes it as the glory of the Son elevates by his saving grace the beauty of the world – it is this Thomas whom Balthasar places at the axis of metaphysics, ancient and modern. Aquinas's thought is the classical and climactic moment which should serve as a paradigm for the whole enterprise of linking philosophical and biblical aesthetics on which Balthasar is engaged.

And why is that? It is because of the way Aquinas shows being as always in process of pouring itself out into the things that are. The glory of being that flows into beings from their source is not unconnected with what we can call being's simultaneous poverty. Being keeps back nothing for itself and has no final resting place save in the actual beings whose act of existing it provides. So, in its self-dispossessing glory it finds its fulfilment in the self-emptying Son of God who in the Incarnation divested himself to the point of death on the Cross, just as, similarly, it finds its ultimate explanation in the mystery of the Holy Trinity revealed by Christ where the Persons pour themselves out for each other in the very act of constituting themselves as who they are.[4]

---

[4] A student of Balthasar who has grasped this with great clarity is André Léonard, now bishop of Namur, in his *Pensées des hommes et foi en Jésus Christ: Pour un discernement intellectuel chrétien* (Paris-Namur 1980), pp. 251-74; 277-88.

Balthasar must now show negatively how we came to decline from this perception, through the sad fate of metaphysics in the West, and, more positively, how through coming to the biblical revelation with new eyes we may be able to recover the perception of glory again.

Already within a century of Thomas's death the Franciscan Scotus and Thomas's fellow-Dominican Eckhart have let the side down. For Scotus, being has just the same rather boring meaning in beings that it has in God. The key Thomistic notion of divinely gifted non-subsistent being as the foundational reality at the heart of all beings, flaring out epiphanically in its selfless reflection of God its Creator, is now abandoned. Being becomes an idea which is at once supreme for it applies to both God and creatures in exactly the same way (something Aquinas would not have dared to assert), and yet almost meaningless, for being is now reduced to a mere registering of this or that's existence.

So, for Balthasar, Scotism anticipated the contemporary scientific outlook at its most banal. What exists are data or facts of which, if he exists, God is simply the largest and most important. In Eckhart, by contrast, being becomes identical with God and creatures lose their full reality. This might seem to be a gain for God, and no doubt Eckhart thought it so, but if God expands to be the reality of everything (he is the All, I am nothing), this cannot but call in question his glory which now has virtually no "space" left in which to manifest itself. So Eckhart – on Balthasar's genealogy of thought – prepares the way for Idealism where reality in its intelligibility becomes a single infinite process neither uncreated nor created or, if you prefer, both at the same time from different standpoints, and so ends up in the abolition of God. As Nietzsche would cry, God is dead, we have killed him – killed him by the progression of our thinking.

How then did people react to the discovery, whether post-Scotist and so ultimately "scientistic" (i.e., pseudo-scientific) or post-Eckhartian and so ultimately Hegelian, that the world has no splendour coming to it in (literally) glorious objectivity from beyond itself? They might try desperately to return to the world of antiquity in the hope that a touch of glory might still be bathing the pagan cosmos, and this is the strategy we find in the Renaissance, with classicism, and in the early Romantics. However, once the infinite God of the biblical revelation had shown up the deities of the ancient pantheon as less than God, there was no real going back. Sooner or later people would find themselves faced with a more radical decision: either nihilism or, in Balthasar's words, "surrender to the sign, in all its purity, of the glory of God's love revealed in Christ".[5]

Here we have a typical trait of Balthasar's thought. The world is irredeemably post-sacred. Through the history of thinking and the feeling which thinking brings in its train, the world has become irreversibly secular (we can think of our own situation where economic and technical innovation, not God, are central to culture) – unless, that is, the gospel be rediscovered. No other religion than Christianity can meet our need, for none other can return glory to being by portraying being as the fruit of the absolute love which the Christ of the Incarnation and Cross has revealed the Trinity to be.

However, Balthasar does not want to persuade us that the history of religious thought since Aquinas is just the story of a two-track disaster leading by two convergent routes, then, to the stupefying either/or question, nihilism or the gospel. For, in his opinion, another kind of experience of glory which also drew from the pagan world and notably from its tragic heroes, and was as authentically Christian as that of Thomas, although not so obviously all-embracing, proved able to develop in a surprising place. Displaced from the life of the cosmos at large, glory took refuge, so to speak, in the hearts of God-filled persons, which is what Balthasar has in mind in speaking, as he now does, of the "metaphysics of the saints". If European Christendom turned away from *esse* (being) in its cosmic manifestation, this had the unexpected advantage of leading people to emphasize the

---

[5] *The Glory of the Lord, V: The Realm of Metaphysics in the Modern Age* (Et Edinburgh 1991), p. 48.

importance of a more immediate – if also somewhat isolated and thus vulnerable – relation to God. In a world which, owing to forgetfulness of *esse*, was a world where the God of glory seemed absent, and thus a tragic world where evil might well appear to have the last word, there was at any rate a compensating possibility of giving greater emphasis to such themes of the gospel as patience, endurance, suffering out of love – in a phrase, the theme of abandoning oneself to God. And what Balthasar tries to show, by setting forth for us the spirituality of a host of figures from the Rhineland mystic John Tauler to the French Jesuit Jean-Pierre de Caussade, is that the self-abandoned person who relies totally on God – the saint – is a kind of personalized version of *esse* in its outpouring, a personalized version of the way in which for Thomas Aquinas being in its dependence on God only consolidates itself in giving itself away to beings. The saint, not the cosmos, in other words, now becomes the epiphany of glory.

What is Balthasar talking about? He is talking about the way in which, beginning in the late medieval period, a picture of what it is to be a saint emerges – a portrait of selfhood as what he terms "total self-giving prodigality", consciously modelled on not only the incarnate atoning Saviour but the Holy Trinity itself. The mystics think of the individual as finding their identity – being him- or her-self – only ecstatically, through going out (*ek-stasis*) in contemplation towards God and in apostolic service towards one's fellow men or women, which "apostolic" ecstasy shows precisely the fruitfulness of the original "contemplative" ecstasy towards God. The mystical saints, therefore, exhibit a form of throwing themselves away lavishly just as does, on the Thomistic view, being itself. What Balthasar would have us see in volume five of *Herrlichkeit* is that the mystics not only guide us to the heart of the biblical revelation but in a sense "solve" the problem of metaphysics. As he writes by way of comment on the Flemish mystic Jan Ruysbroeck, the behaviour and experience which flow from this encounter with God is

> not only the supremely free bestowal of God's grace and thus
> the centre of theology. It is also what gives meaning and

fulfilment to spiritual nature and is consequently the centre of metaphysics. [6]

Christian philosophy *as lived* is summed up in holy fools: the Don Quixote of Cervantes, the Prince Myshkin of Dostoevsky's *The Idiot*. Perfect fools: this is where in our post-medieval Western tradition theological aesthetics takes up its abode.

And yet Balthasar also recognizes that we cannot simply leave the cosmos as a more or less meaningless stage on which meaningful human acts are by exceptional people occasionally performed. It is not enough for the self-giving glory of God to manifest itself at these few scattered points; we need to know as well that it really is the universal foundation of the whole world and its history.

And that is why in the concluding volumes Balthasar turns again to the Bible in the hope that – now we grasp what is at stake in theological aesthetics – we can read Scripture afresh. If we do so in the light of these concerns, we shall perhaps see how, through the New Testament's amazing consummation of the Old, the mystery of all creation, man included, received its definitive interpretation as the hidden presence of absolute love, to which in its luminous, bountiful and exuberant character beauty's qualities of clarity, integrity and proportion by analogy belong. See too how the recipients of God's self-revelation – ourselves – receive thereby the call to make the divine visible in charity, the specifically Christian love of neighbour which is, as Balthasar puts it

> something quite distinct from a good and morally upright model for inter-personal conduct. [This love] occurs always as the focal point, as the demonstration and realization of a love which itself wholly transcends man, and thus also as an indicator of that love which man cannot ascribe to himself since it has long since showed itself to him as that which is ever greater than himself.[7]

---

[6] Ibid., p. 68.
[7] Ibid., p. 649.

"Ever-greater", *je grösser, semper maior* – that refers to the inexhaustible, self-dispossessing energy of the Triune love, which was pointed to in the prophets of the Old Covenant, those servants in whom Yahweh expressed his burning passion, but which at the turn of the ages was actually manifested, beyond all human expectation, in the mission of the Son, whose incarnation, death and descent into Hell flesh out for us in the art of a divine narrative the very essence of the Holy Trinity, the absolute love which God is and in which Christ's glory too consists, as the Easter mysteries tell us each year in the Liturgy of the Church.

The Incarnation and Atonement – this is the message of the closing volumes of *Herrlichkeit* – resolve the central issue of all aesthetics: how an infinite significance can be found through a finite vehicle, and *what* a significance it turns out to be! In Jesus, the image of God which for Israel is man, and the glory of God which for Israel is God himself, come wondrously to coincide, and the unfolding of Jesus's story – his life, death and Resurrection – exhibits to us what that is going to mean if God's glory really is his unconditional love now freely exposing itself in vulnerable fashion to a sinful world.

And this is how Balthasar himself sums up the aim of *Herrlichkeit* at large in his essay *Rechenschaft*. The goal of the theological aesthetics was

> to let us see the revelation of God that his lordliness, his sublimity, what Israel calls *kabod* ("glory") and the New Testament *gloria* can be recognized under all the incognitos of the human nature [of Christ] and [his] Cross. That means [Balthasar concluded] God comes not primarily as our teacher or as our purposeful redeemer but *for himself* – to show forth and radiate out what is splendid in his eternal triune love in that disinterestedness which true love has in common with true beauty.[8]

In E.M. Forster's novel *Howard's End*, we read:

---

[8] Cited from *Mein Werk*, p.62.

> "But this is something quite new", said Mrs Munt, who collected new ideas as a squirrel collects nuts and was especially attracted by those that are portable.[9]

This essay may have included nuts, but how far they can be carried into the wider wood of Anglo-Saxon culture remains an open question. Balthasar himself, in *Epilog*, questioned how much use his entire trilogy of aesthetics, dramatics and logic was going to be to a Church that is often as activist and unthoughtful as the culture it inhabits. He offered his theology, he said, in the spirit of someone putting a message in a bottle and throwing it overboard from a boat in mid-ocean. That such a bottle land and someone find its message is, he commented, something of a miracle, adding, *Aber zuweilen geschehen solche,* "But sometimes such things happen".[10]

---

[9] E.M. Forster, *Howard's End*, ed. O. Stallybrass (Harmondsworth 1983), p. 72.

[10] *Epilog*, p. 8. A book-length (and so less pointed) reading of *Herrlichkeit* is found in the present author's *The Word Has Been Abroad: A Guide through Balthasar's Aesthetics* (Edinburgh 1998).

VI

RAHNER AND BALTHASAR:

THE ANONYMOUS CHRISTIANITY
DEBATE REVISITED

The criticisms which Hans Urs von Balthasar levelled at Karl Rahner's concept of "anonymous Christianity" are hardly a *bagatelle*, for three reasons. First, they seem to query the legitimacy of Rahnerianism as a Catholic theology – its right to be a player in the orchestra of theological pluralism in the Church. For, on the one hand, despite the relatively modest place, quantitatively speaking, that such ideas as "anonymous Christianity", "anonymous faith", "anonymous discipleship" occupy in Rahner's corpus,[1] many Rahner commentators would agree that these concepts nonetheless exhibit in a way no others do the inherent theological dynamic of Rahner's thought.[2] And on the other hand, Balthasar's criticism of them appears to be not that they need modification in some fashion or re-contextualisation in some wider perspective but that they are, quite simply, contradictions in terms, or, more specifically, examples of *contradictio in adjecto* where the adjective ("anonymous") unconditionally nullifies the content entertained by the noun ("Christianity", "faith", "discipleship"). Then secondly, it is alleged that the currency given these terms and the mind-set they exemplify, by the prestige attaching to Rahner's name as one of the great masters of twentieth century Catholic theology not least at the Second Vatican Council, has not simply damaged *theological*

---

[1] Beginning in 1960 with "Poetry and the Christian" (*Theological Investigations* IV, Et London 1966), p. 366, the concept is mentioned in as many, however, as sixteen succeeding volumes of the series.

[2] Notably, the meaning of the "supernatural existential": see on this K.-H. Weger, *Karl Rahner: An Introduction to his Theology* (Et London 1980), p. 113.

culture, the thinking found within the Church. More alarmingly still it has adversely affected *ecclesial practice*, the action which Catholics feel committed to by virtue of their faith. Notably, the "anonymous Christianity" notion has severed, at any rate partially, that nerve of the mystical Body which connects the Body to missionary activity – evangelism, the seeking of conversions, the spreading of the faith. Thirdly, if it is true to say that Rahnerism and Balthasarianism are the two most influential forms of Catholic theology found today in the "first world", then the existence of what is little less than a state of civil war between their adherents diminishes the unity of the Church, at least in the sense of lowering the tone of ecclesial communion – something acutely felt in Germanophone Catholicism at the present time, and more widely reflected in the *querelle des journaux*, between adherents of *Concilium* and protagonists of *Communio*.

In this essay I shall first expound Balthasar's critique of the "anonymous Christianity" concept, noting how this critique appears mainly in Balthasar's shorter controversial and occasional writings (though it is also present more allusively, and perhaps serenely, in his principal theological writings – notably the great "trilogy" of the theological aesthetics, theological dramatics and theological logic). Next, I will outline the foundations of the "anonymous Christianity" notion in Rahner's treatment of the ideas of revelation and faith. Finally, I will attempt an adjudication, with the aim, in part, of suggesting ways in which the alarming gap separating Rahnerian from Balthasarian thought can be narrowed, and the negative effects of the conflict between these parties mitigated though by no means entirely removed.

Writing chiefly, as already mentioned, in his shorter, more polemical and even journalistic pieces, and beginning in 1963, Balthasar, while admitting Rahner's great gifts and the contribution he had made to a number of disputed questions in Catholic theology,[3] nevertheless considered that Rahner's emerging

---

[3] Note, for instance, the handsome tribute Balthasar wrote for Rahner's sixtieth birthday ("Karl Rahner. Zum 60. Geburtstag", *Neue Zürcher Nachrichten* 28, *Beilage Christliche Kultur*, 9), and the way he is capable of bracketing him with his beloved

system *taken as a whole* was betraying the very substance of the Christian religion in its Catholic form. Rahner had treated philosophy, and notably the "transcendental" philosophy derived from combining the Idealism of Kant and Fichte with the realism of Aristotle and Aquinas, as not simply a useful adjunct to the theological enterprise but as able, in and of itself, to provide a structure of thought which could adequately express the Christian mystery. He had taken the guts out of Christian soteriology (the doctrine of salvation) in general, and staurology (the theology of the Cross) in particular, by proposing that the saved person owes their redemption not to Christ but to the eternal saving will of God which becomes recognisable in the life of Christ – *im Existenzvollzug Christi*. But is it not the case, Balthasar asked, that Christ's life, death and Resurrection (but above all his death) actually *achieved* our salvation? Can it suffice to say that the "Christ-event" simply made our salvation known? Will it really do to say of the death of Christ that it shows salvation taking irreversible hold on humankind in one unique yet representative case, as Christ surrenders himself into the hands of a loving Father, such that his death becomes exemplary for how we too should enter eternity? After all, Balthasar remarks, as much (or as little) could be said by a Catholic Christian of the death Mary died in her Dormition. Again, – continuing the catalogue of Balthasar's complaints – Rahner has reduced the love of God to love of neighbour, not only taking up an anthropological starting-point but also coming to an anthropocentric conclusion, where love of neighbour becomes the fundamental act of human self-transcendence whereby I not only implicitly orientate myself towards the God who is man's ultimate "horizon" (a favoured Rahnerian term), but (equally implicitly) accept God's redeeming grace and am saved. He has sundered the Gospel from what is, for the New Testament, its single most important practical consequence: martyrdom, apostolic suffering for the *Name* of the

---

mentor Henri de Lubac: "men who know how to awaken unhoped-for timely living substance from what [in 'decayed theologies'] seemed to be dead", *Convergences: To the Source of Christian Mystery* (Et San Francisco 1983), p.12.

Lord Jesus Christ, that explicit confession by which the Christian, in fact though not in Rahner's theology, is drawn into both the life and the death of the Saviour.[4] As Balthasar himself puts it:

> He who speaks of "anonymous Christianity" cannot (and will not wish to) avoid an ultimate univocity between Christians with the Name and Christians without. Consequently, despite all subsequent protests, it cannot be of importance whether or not one confesses the Name. [Just as] he who presents love of God and love of neighbour as identical, and the love of neighbour as the primary act of the love of God, may not be (and probably is not) surprised if it becomes a matter of indifference whether people confess belief in God or not.[5]

And in a reply to critics of the book in which these words occur he went on to describe his purpose in querying Rahnerianism as being

> to ask Christians, and theologians among them, if they were prepared to shed their blood, in the sense of the Gospel and as the ancient Church understood it, for the incarnate God who bore the sins of the world and also yours and mine.[6]

Rahner appeared to be using, for most of the time, the same language as the dogmatic tradition but he had in fact substituted new meanings which eviscerated those terms of their content. Balthasar calls this *Ausweitung*: "stretching" dogma beyond what is, when considered as interpretation of the historic Christian tradition, at all credible. (Balthasar did not deny that Rahner's version might be currently more credible in terms of the question defined by Mgr. Ronald Knox as "How much can Jones swallow?".)

Moreover, while Rahner thought that the great philosophies and world religions might involve what he termed a "pre-grasp"

---

[4] Balthasar was thinking of, e.g., "The Commandment of Love in Relation to the Other Commandments", *Theological Investigations* V (Et London 1966) pp.439-459; "Reflections on the Unity of the Love of Neighbour and the Love of God", ibid. VI (Et London 1974), pp. 231-249; *Foundation of Christian Faith* (Et London 1978), pp. 456-457.

[5] *Cordula oder der Ernstfall* (Einsiedeln 1967²), p. 103.

[6] "Apologia pro Cordula sua", *Civitas* 22 (1966-1967), p. 441.

(*Vorgriff*) or tacit anticipation of God's free self-disclosure in saving grace, Balthasar considered it more prudent to regard both sets of phenomena (he held the non-Abrahamic world religions to be philosophies by another name) as, at best, expressing humanity's yearning for truth and wisdom, and, at worst, particularly clear manifestations of original sin, distracting men from ultimate questions, or encouraging resignation to the apparent sheer meaninglessness of existence, or deluding people into thinking they have found answers to the crucial questions – and in all these ways frustrating, or at least hindering, God's outreach to his creatures.

We must think too, so Balthasar insists, of the possible implications of the "anonymous Christianity" idea for ecclesiology. Is the Church nothing more than the explicit expression of what is already a hidden reality outside her? Is she simply what Rahner termed

> the historically tangible vanguard, and the historically and socially constituted explicit expression of what the Christian hopes is present as a hidden reality even outside the visible Church.[7]?

Is it only the explicitation of a tacit dimension that makes the Church different from the world?

And above all, and this is perhaps the key to all of the *gravamina* against Rahner I have cited from Balthasar's works: Is it right to think of the simple openness of the human mind or spirit (*Geist*) to a supernatural horizon, to the prospect of God's supernatural self-communication of his own life, as itself *already* an experience of grace? And if, with Rahner, we think it *is* right, then does not this state of affairs – what Rahner, famously, called the "supernatural existential" – do away with the need for an historical revelation at all? Is it sufficient to defend the existence and continuing pertinence of the historical revelation by saying that, by means of it, human beings become *consciously aware* of the

---

[7] "Christianity and Non-Christian Religions", in *Theological Investigations* V, op. cit., p. 133.

fulfilment in love they have always been offered all the time. As Balthasar puts it:

> My main argument... is this: It might be true that from the very beginning man was created to be disposed towards God's revelation... *Gratia supponit naturam.* But when God's grace sends his own living Word to his creatures, he does not do so... primarily to fulfil their deepest needs and yearnings. Rather he communicates and actively demonstrates such unheard-of things that man feels not so much satisfied as awestruck by a love which he could never have hoped to experience. For who would dare to have described God as love, without having first received the revelation of the Trinity in the acceptance of the Cross by the Son?[8]

The idea of "anonymous Christianity" is, then, a focus, on Balthasar's view, for an inter-related series of errors in Christian thinking: whether in fundamental theology, as with the belief that a transcendental philosophy can anticipate the distinctive content of Christian revelation; or in soteriology, where the life, death and Resurrection of Christ become exemplary rather than efficacious in force; or in theological ethics where the love of neighbour becomes a surrogate for the love of God and Christological confession no longer necessary for Christian existence; or in the theology of religions which become in fact if not in name ordinary ways of salvation alongside the Christian way; or in ecclesiology where the Church becomes simply the explicit articulation of what is equally present (though only implicitly so) wherever the world opens itself to the Kingdom; or finally in the theology of history where the universal openness of the human spirit to divine transcendence in its supernatural offer of salvation is already deemed to be *Gnadenerfahrung,* "the experience of grace", even without any further intervention of the redeeming God in the special history of revelation – and so salvation – found in Israel, in Jesus Christ, and in the Church he founded.

Now this is, evidently, a formidable indictment, but as remarked earlier it is, I think, significant that most of it is to be

---

[8] H. U. von Balthasar, "Current Trends in Catholic Theology and the Responsibility of the Christian", *Communio* 5 (1978), p. 79.

found in Balthasar's *opuscula*, his occasional and notably polemical pieces, rather than in the principal works. And the reason for that is, I believe, that his target was chiefly what can be called "vulgarised Rahnerianism" – an attitude of mind among theologically literate, or at least religiously articulate, Catholics which owed much, certainly, to Rahner but on the way had shed much too in the way of nuance and qualification.

That not all Balthasar's criticisms meet their mark, or at any rate not all to the same degree, where Rahner's own theology is concerned seems (to anticipate) more than likely. That is not to say, however, that absolutely all is well with a type of theology Balthasar by no means unjustifiably described as German Idealism in baptised form.[9]

How, then, does the concept of the "anonymous Christian" arise in Rahner's thought? Rahner was convinced that in a civilization dominated by humanism the only possible starting-point for Christian theology is anthropological – one that can show how God is necessary to man. The only kind of anthropology that will serve theology's turn, however, is a transcendental one – one, that is, which shows God as already somehow implicated in lived humanity, enabling its very possibility. (The word "transcendental" in this context is drawn from Kant in whose thought it denotes those prior structures or features of a thing which make its activity – usually its knowing activity – possible.) It was to this task that his two most sustained exercises in philosophical theology – *Spirit in the World*, a study in ontological metaphysics, and *Hearers of the Word*, an anthropology written within the perspective of fundamental theology – were devoted.[10] Under the influence of the early Heidegger who had defined man as the questioning animal who asks most notably, Why is there something rather than nothing?, and concerned to preserve his links via Jesuit Scholasticism with the tradition of Aristotelean Thomism, Rahner soon decided that the only possible

---

[9] H. U. von Balthasar, "In Retrospect", *Communio* (Winter 1975), p. 200.

[10] *Spirit in the World* (Et London 1968; 1979); *Hearers of the Word* (Et London 1969).

starting-point for a transcendental anthropology was the pervasive fact that human beings ask about the whole, ask what everything is all about, thus raising the question of the *being* of the particular beings that there are, what they have in common, what inter-relates them. For Balthasar, such opting for a philosophical point of departure already made inevitable a certain relativization of biblical revelation: the philosophical vision makes the *Gedankenführung*, the "way thought proceeds", lose something of the freshness and immediacy of the biblical Word.[11] Be that as it may, the "pervasive fact" in question was called by Rahner (following Heidegger) an "existential" – an inescapable dimension of human existence, soaking our experience through and through. From this he drew the conclusion (and here is where the influence of the developed Idealism of Fichte shows its hand[12]) that since being is fundamentally open to man there is what Rahner termed an a priori unity of being and knowing. Knowing is the *Beisichsein des Seins* – the way being is at home with itself. And so both knowing and being are essentially subjecthood or self-possession.[13] However, because being, for us, is questionable – that was the transcendental anthropological stand-point we originally took up in phenomenologically analysing the human condition – there must be, evidently, differing extents to which a being can possess being and so be at home with being as a whole. Because the human spirit's hold on being is not complete, that spirit finds itself bound to the world, to what is not itself. But this is, more positively, a golden opportunity for *Geist*, for that same spirit which via the other, via the world, can come to a fuller grasp of itself, and so of the being which, as knowing spirit, it fundamentally is. And since that is so, the human spirit is essentially sensuous spirit, sense-bound spirit, since for Rahner

---

[11] "Grösse und Last der Theologie heute: Einige grundsätzliche Gedanken zu zwei Aufsatzbänden Karl Rahners *Schriften zur Theologie*, Einsiedeln-Zürich", *Wort und Wahrheit* 10 (1955), pp.531-533.

[12] P. Eicher, *Die anthropologische Wende: Karl Rahners philosophischer Weg vom Wesen des Menschen zur personalen Existenz* (Freiburg in der Schweiz 1970), pp. 205-207.

[13] A claim subjected, from a Thomist standpoint, to sharp criticism in C. Fabro, *La Svolta antropologica di Karl Rahner* (Milan 1974), pp. 46-87.

"sensuousness", *Sinnlichkeit*, does not refer, as it would in a more robustly realist metaphysical context, primarily to the physical, corporeal realm, but to what he calls the "surrenderedness of being, which is subjecthood, to the other" (*die Hingegebenheit des Seins, das Beisichsein ist, an das andere*). Rahner would maintain that such necessity of reference to another, to what is other than myself, is the chief meaning of being embodied.

In Aristotelian Thomism, when the other is grasped by me as an object that truly pertains to the real, I make a judgment, expressed in the copula, that this *is* such-and-such: an act which Rahner describes as my exercising a capacity for *ein Vorgriff* which is specifically not a *Begriff*, a concept that I entertain, but (literally) a "pre-grasp" (an anticipation) of the wider horizon of being, and ultimately of unconditional or absolute being, in whose perspective I place myself in knowing the object. (Here we see Rahner, in a way typical of Idealism, attempting to deduce the reality of the Absolute from the human spirit's openness thereto.) Rahner goes on to say that, since in knowing I do not merely note the existence of something but take (albeit tacitly) the measure of its grasp of being – the extent to which it possesses being (for as between, say, a pebble and a person this can vary enormously), the *Vorgriff* equips me with a preliminary grasp of the differentiated, structured character of conditioned or contingent being, all being that falls short of the absolute, the unconditional, the necessary. Human knowledge takes place, then, by a turning to the world in knowing via the senses and in a return of the human spirit to itself – because it was for the sake of completing my "at-homeness" with being that, like everyone else, I launched myself into the world of otherness in the first place. This could be pure St Thomas, the *conversio ad phantasmata* ("turning to the images") on the one hand, the *reditio completa in seipsum* ("completed return to oneself") on the other, but where, once again, Rahner shows his Idealist inheritance is in the further remark that these two moments of knowing are chiefly united through the fact that the human spirit is the source of the sensuousness which enables it to return to itself: as Rahner puts it, it is the quasi-formal cause of the sensuousness of the body. The spirit which has the images of all things in potentiality within itself (an Idealist rendering of the Thomist doctrine that *anima quodammodo omnia*, "the soul is in a certain way all things") at one and the same time makes the sensuous what it is in its innermost constitution, here acting as its formal cause, but also remains utterly free in its regard – which is what we are meant to understand by the addition of that qualifying "quasi".

None of this is to say, however, that the way human beings perceive the world may not vary in different epochs, for the spirit can be thought of not only in its a priori structure (just described), which is, certainly, always one and the same (or there would not be a unitary humankind), and not simply in the way it performs a discreet act of concrete knowing, but *also in its relation to its previous accumulated acts of knowledge at large.* In this latter sense, the spirit can take a variety of forms (*Gestalten*) in the course of history – history both corporate and individually biographical. For spirit is not only spontaneous, it is also receptive. It is not simply constitutive of other realities but also affected by them, though by way of its own act. In the most important consequence of this for our subject: the "horizon" of being displayed in the *Vorgriff* can present itself to the human spirit by forming that spirit in different ways. As history unfolds there can be various *Gestalten* of transcendence, and therefore a genuine history of transcendence – which we must not imagine, on the basis of human nature alone, to be always the same. And this is a crucial step, for Rahner will go on to say that, in point of revealed fact, God has not only altered the dynamism of the human spirit from which this whole analysis set out, so that it now aims, whether successfully or not, at a supernaturally heightened goal, what Rahner calls a supernaturally elevated transcendentality. Moreover, in what is at any rate a sustainable interpretation of Rahner's thought, God *provides in the course of salvation history different forms (Gestalten) of being actively related to that goal, different kinds of human experience of transcendence as ways of appropriating that supernatural transcendentality.*[14]

So whereas by nature (and therefore universally) man, for Rahner, needs an "horizon" for his knowing activity, and thanks to the unbounded character of that horizon can open himself in an anticipatory sort of way to what Rahner terms the "absolute having of being" (*die absolute Seinshabe*, corresponding, in his theology, to the *actus purus* of St Thomas), and this is, from Adam to the Apocalypse, *formally* speaking, the situation of everyone, nonetheless we are not to suppose that *materially* the content of this "horizon" – and so the character of the transcendental goal that is offered man, and the different forms that offer can take – remain, in the varying epochs of salvation history one and the same (or even, in all respects, the same *within* such an epoch for one individual human being compared with another). And since supernatural transcendality means, in plain English, God's gift of himself – for Rahner, like Balthasar, and the Dogmatic Constitution *Dei Verbum* of the Second Vatican Council, regards revelation as primarily God's communication of his own life (which is why, to both these thinkers, the concepts of revelation and salvation are theologically inseparable) – then God can give himself in different *Gestalten*, "in many and various ways", as the opening of the Letter to the Hebrews has it.

For Rahner, God does in point of fact thus reveal himself through what he calls *Realsymbolen*, "real symbols".[15] Putting forth an expression of oneself as a way of taking possession of oneself is not, in Rahner's eyes, simply a sign of creaturely finitude and imperfection but belongs with the foundational structure of any reality characterised by unity. Indeed, the archetype of *Realsymbolik* is in God where the Father generates his own Logos, and loves that Word as his self-expression in the Holy Spirit. Because the "real symbol" is also the self-expression of any being

---

[14] K.P. Fischer, *Gotteserfahrung: Mystagogie in der Theologie Karl Rahners und in der Theologie der Befreiung* (Mainz 1986), pp. 68-72.

[15] J.H.P. Wong, *Logos-Symbol in the Christology of Karl Rahner* (Rome 1984) is especially good on this – as Rahner himself acknowledged in a preface.

within the triunely created world, encounter with whatever shares in being is always mediated by its "symbol". And every being, however lowly, has its real "symbol"(s) in which it is quasi-formally present (making that expression the expression it is, in other words, but not as though it were entirely invested in it). But since the reality thus "symbolised" is for the first time truly itself in its "symbol", Rahner can speak of the "symbol" – disconcertingly, at first sight – as the "cause" of the "symbolised", just as in the Holy Trinity, the Father only becomes Father in the (eternal) generation of the Son as they spirate (everlastingly) their common Breath. And this is all *philosophically* relevant, for rational freedom cannot exclude the possibility that absolute Being, God – who is for Rahner implicitly co-affirmed, *mit-bejaht*, in our anticipatory grasp, in all knowing, of the rich totality of being – could by revealing himself modify the horizon in which our experience of transcendence takes place, putting forth real symbols of his new mode of self-manifestation, real symbols which, then, would be, in the sense explained, the causes of this new state of affairs. Because of their openness to transcendence, human beings, in the *de facto* situation of the supernatural economy in which creation finds itself, can be not only receptive to being but also *hearers of the Word*. What men and women actually encounter in that capacity, however, is not the new supernatural transcendentality itself (or even the form of transcendence in which it gives itself) but rather its "symbol" – the finite self-expression which Rahner calls, borrowing this key-term too from Kant, "categorial", meaning: the concrete object by whose means in a posteriori fashion we register what the a priori transcendental conditions of possibility of our knowledge enable us to understand.

Categorial experience might seem less significant than transcendental, yet for Rahner categorial objects can have horizon-opening and horizon-changing power, given the way that (as we have seen) the sensuous can determine spirit, where spirit in its freedom allows that to happen. The categorial objects of whose cognition our direct experience is composed can play a major part, then, in *man's* "revelation" of himself to himself as spirit in the world. The later Rahner will stress increasingly the *conversio ad phantasmata* not as a turning to the sensuous in general but as, more specifically, a turning to *human history*. Indeed, for Rahner, as Werner Schreer has put it, history is essentially an "interpersonal, real-symbolic transaction between transcendentality and categoriality".[16] *But* those same categorial objects, given their candidacy as possible "real symbols" for divine self-expressiveness, can *also* play a part, even more importantly, in *God's* self-revelation to man – in the history, then, of *salvation*. Some have detected, indeed, a healthful development in Rahner's thinking here. The tendency of his early and middle period (what Vincent Holzer calls "the first Rahner") to treat Christology as an exemplification of the relation between God and history yields in his final years to the desire to restore to Christology "an epiphanic dimension" – even if the join between the aboriginal divine self-giving to human freedom and this Christological mediation of the divine life is by no means cleanly made.[16a]

It follows nonetheless – and here we reach a juncture where the conflict between Rahner and Balthasar cannot be smoothed over – that Rahner's true focus of interest is concentrated not on the "real symbol" but on the human interiority which it can affect, for in his view human transcendence – that is, the dynamism of spirit – is the only point in the world which intersects with being at large, and so with God. Strictly speaking, therefore, revelation is found not in the "real symbol", but in the way the latter alters the horizon of human transcendence. Though man's supernatural transcendental experience be impossible without the categorial objects that not only occasion it but give it a peculiar stamp all its own in some particular historical epoch in the economy of salvation, nonetheless revelation itself is essentially the *interpretation* of that experience.

---

[16] W. Schreer, *Der Begriff des Glaubens: Das Verständnis des Glaubensaktes in den Dokumenten des Vatikanum II und in den theologischen Entwürfen Karl Rahners und Hans Urs von Balthasars* (Frankfurt 1992), p. 283.

[16a] V. Holzer, *Le Dieu Trinité dans l'histoire: Le différend théologique Balthasar-Rahner* (Paris 1995), p. 25.

Now, according to Rahner, the idea of the Incarnation as the high point of all such historical revelation is already implicit in transcendental experience – even, were it ever to have existed in isolation, that of a purely natural kind. (This is his Christologically oriented version of St Thomas' notion of the natural desire for the vision of God.) Since everyone, as *Geist*, aspires to a perfected hold on being, he or she tacitly practises *suchende Christologie*, "a priori Christology". The idea of the historical mediation – the appearing in our midst – of the transcendental self-communication of absolute Being (that is, the idea of the God-man) is the same as that of the promise of full possession of being. It is the notion of the human being in whom the search for absolute Being comes to its goal. And so to entertain the "idea" of Christ is to conceive a correlative, at the categorial level, of the transcendental structure of human being and knowing in its achieved state. The concept of *der absolute Heilsbringer*, the carrier of definitive salvation, is the idea of one who, by virtue of his whole existence – including, then, his death – remains the visible – which must mean, for a dead man, the *risen* – promise to the seeker of a perfect hold on being, a promise namely that his or her quest or hope is not in vain. In this sense, the high point of Christian revelation (and here Balthasar's reading of Rahner is quite correct) simply confirms what any human being tacitly expects or at least hopes for, what he or she anonymously entertains.

But – and this could be overlooked – as the "real symbol" of God's desire to unite himself unshakeably to humankind, Jesus Christ in his life, death and resurrection, exercises *Symbolursächlichkeit*: Jesus Christ is, in those events, the "symbolic cause" of the divine engagement to engrace the world found in the de facto supernaturally elevated created order. He is the cause of God's universally saving intention, which intention, for Rahner, only comes to itself on the Cross of Christ.

> Thus in Christ God's love-creating condescension becomes irreversible and unequivocally accessible in the salvation

history of the world, because through the Cross the Holy
Spirit is sent into the hearts of all men and women.[17]

At the same time, like any categorial object of real-symbolic epoch-
making force, the Christ-event opens up the new horizon that
makes all awareness of the possibility of such "anonymous
Christianity" available in the first place. In so doing, it brings with
it a new *Transzendenzgestalt*. The supernatural existential is itself
Christologically structured, not only in the sense that the
ordination of the world to God is caused by Christ (in the way
already explained), and that all grace is, therefore, *gratia Christi*,
but also in the further sense that only after the Christ-event can
the scope of this existential be consciously grasped.

Ideally (in the common or garden sense of that word!),
someone living in the culminating Christian epoch of the world's
history should be a Christian: the transcendental and categorial
aspects of revelation ought not to be sundered. That does not
mean, however, Rahner explains, that no surrogates for the
categorial object which is Jesus Christ as presented by the Church's
tradition can be found. It would be the office of such surrogates
to give the new form of transcendence entry into non-believers'
lives. In fact, so Rahner thought, God offers saving grace wherever
he creates the conditions of possibility for that grace's acceptance,
by the providential provision of such surrogate objects which open
up, for Tom, Dick or Harriet, the horizon of supernatural
transcendence in the form appropriate to the era inaugurated by
the victorious Cross.

The Father is revealed categorially in the Son made man,
but transcendentally in the Spirit, and so must furnish for the
person who is, through no fault of his own, an unbeliever,
anonymous opportunities to practise, through the Spirit, "faith" in
and "discipleship" of the unrecognised Son. The three chief
surrogates Rahner considers in this connexion are: first, readiness
for death; secondly, hope for the future; and third, love of

---

[17] E. Conway, *The Anonymous Christian – a Relativised Christianity? An Evaluation of
Hans Urs von Balthasar's Criticisms of Karl Rahner's Theory of the Anonymous Christian*
(Frankfurt 1990), p. 103.

neighbour, for in all three we are dealing with a "wager" of one's own existence only possible, he thinks, by a kind of grace-supported faith. God's love for, and acceptance of, humankind, irreversibly confirmed in Jesus Christ, constitutes the sole basis whereby we can take the risk of abandoning ourselves unreservedly and (especially) of loving unconditionally. Of Rahner's trio, the love of neighbour, then, appears to be the central surrogate from which midpoint the others should be interpreted. Thanks to his or her "transcendentality" simply as a human being, the neighbour is always a "real symbol" – in the language of Genesis 1, 26, "in the image and likeness" – of God.

Just as, for Rahner, secular history is simply co-extensive with the general (though not the special) history of revelation and salvation – and this, he thought, justified him in regarding anything in the history of the cosmos as a *possible* quasi-object of faith (a mediation of the true formal object of faith, God himself), so for him there are no exclusively secular human acts, actions with an ethical but not salvific charge, since all can somehow be related to the order of love of neighbour: from which it follows that any good moral action is a quasi-act of faith, a moment when, even if we be atheists, we can receive justifying grace and enjoy supernatural sanctification.

Balthasar's question, "Why then go to the trouble of explicit believing?" at once arises. To Rahner, that question was misplaced. By its own dynamism the spirit always seeks to narrow down the distance between its transcendental orientation and the "real-symbolic" expression of that orientation with which it has to do. Of its nature, then, it tends necessarily to explicit faith.

> The faith as it exists in the pagan is properly speaking designed to follow its own inherent dynamism in such a way as to develop into that faith which we simply call the Christian faith. The seed has no right to seek not to grow into a plant.[18]

Anonymous believers *eo ipso* are required to seek explicit faith in Christ – what Rahner terms the "sealing of their hope", and that

---

[18] *Theological Investigations* XIV (Et London 1976), p. 291.

hope's "historical and unconditional guarantee". Were they to renounce this search they would falsify the essence of faith and so cease to be anonymous believers at all. Moreover, thanks to the principle of the mutual interaction of categorial and transcendental, the explicit object of faith, Jesus Christ, has the power to change the life of the one who comes to explicit confession. Here Rahner would speak of such factors in living as: renewed courage, spiritual peace, a more demanding call to conversion of life, increase of confidence in the fundamental option already taken in anonymous faith, the greater chance of anonymous (putative) discipleship truly being a transcendental experience of the grace of Christ when its own categorial content is correct, and, not least, access to the visible form of grace in the Church, continuing as she does in corporate fashion the "real symbolic" function of the incarnate Word. In sum:

> The individual who grasps Christianity in a clearer, purer and more reflective way has, other things being equal, a still greater chance of salvation than someone who is merely an anonymous Christian.[19]

And yet – alas! – we can also find Rahner suppressing, or at least neglecting, the nuances of his own theory, as when in the fifth volume of the *Investigations* he writes

> I see nothing other in my Christianity than the explicit home-coming of everything in the way of truth and love which exists or could exist anywhere.[20]

Balthasar would readily admit that the problem of the salvation of the unbeliever is, for Christian theology, perfectly real. The mediaeval doctrine of the saving significance of the desire for Baptism, confirmed at Trent, and the 1949 Letter of the Holy Office to the archbishop of Boston which, in the course of its condemnation of the unfortunate Father Leonard Feeney, spoke of the soteriological value, moreover, of even an implicit form of such desire, bear witness to the Church's attempt to address the issue

---

[19] *Theological Investigations* V, op. cit., p. 132.
[20] Ibid., p. 9.

with generosity of spirit. [21] One could go back further into the Tradition, to Justin Martyr's statement in the *First Apology* (I. 46) that "those who lived according to the Logos were Christians even if they were considered atheists", or Augustine's assertion in the *Retractations* (I. 13. 3) that "what is now called the Christian religion was there in the past and was never unknown from the beginning of humanity up to Christ's coming in the flesh". That is pertinent background to the claim of the Pastoral Constitution of the Second Vatican Council on the Church in the Modern World, that

> since Christ died for all and since all men are in fact called to one and the same destiny, which is divine, we must hold that the Holy Spirit offers to all the possibility of being made partners, in a way known to God, in the paschal mystery...[22]

Let us note, however, that the Church has never pretended to be able to identify "surrogates" which constitute media of salvation with the confidence shown by Rahner, and that the consensus of her divines in times past has been rather to respect, as the minimum content of any faith that could justify, the words of Hebrews 11, 6: "Whoever would draw near to God must believe that he exists and that he rewards those who seek him". Not that Balthasar, who in his last years was accused of crypto-universalism for daring to hope that all human beings might be saved, can be accused or reneging on this particular conciliar text. What he

---

[21] Rahner commented acutely on this in *Theological Investigations* XII (Et London 1974), pp. 171-172:
"The theologians did not in the least feel it to be any objection to ask how in that case the sacrament was still necessary and meaningful, seeing that the *res sacramenti*, the justification, is already conferred even before the reception of the sacrament. Manifestly in their theology of saving history and grace at the collective and individual levels it was obvious to them that the signs of grace as found in the historical dimension and in the Church were not rendered superfluous and meaningless by the fact that grace is already prior to them for there is an incarnational order such that this grace itself of its very nature seeks its historical embodiment in the world and above all in the sacrament, so that it itself would be denied if an individual sought in principle to frustrate this incarnational dynamism inherent in grace itself."

[22] *Gaudium et Spes*, 22.

stressed, however, was, in the first instance, the words *in modo Deo cognito*, "in a way known to God" (rather than "in a way known only to Rahner"!). In both the theological aesthetics and the theological dramatics he speaks of the possibility of an inchoative faith, founded on the mysterious iridescence of the uncreated Being of the Creator in the "form" (*Gestalt*) of the creation. How far that sort of faith actually characterises some individuals and brings them to salvation is not disclosed to us. It is not, he maintained, a duty of Christians to theorise about the salvation of unbelievers. Indeed, the Saviour himself warned against it – at least on Balthasar's interpretation of the pericope in John 21 where Peter asks what will become of the beloved disciple. On Balthasar's reading, the Fourth Evangelist here takes up the question left hanging in the air by the committal to Peter of the office of loving care for the sheep – namely, outside the visible communion of the Church, will love endure? But Jesus replies, "If I will that he should abide till my coming, what is that to you? Follow me." (Jn 21: 22).[23] In other words, the Christian has to live out his faith, which includes, on Balthasar's view, hoping for the salvation of all: that is more than sufficient to occupy his time. Here we have a response to Rahner partly theological – an apophatic reminder of the limits of our understanding and the consequent need for restraint and discretion – and partly pastoral, guided by Balthasar's conviction that the dissemination of Rahner's theologoumenon has damaged the Catholic Church's sense of uniqueness, and so of identity, and therefore of mission.

More concentratedly theological is Balthasar's insistence that if hypotheses are to be presented in order to investigate, in all reverence, what that hidden way, unstated in revelation and in the Church's teaching, of sharing in the Paschal Mystery might be, this must not be allowed to sell short the distinctive truth-claims of the actual revelation which is, *pace* Rahner, the only one we have. Specifically, the scope of that revelation must not be restricted to a matter of fulfilling the yearnings, hopes and

---

[23] *Convergences*, op. cit., pp. 72-73.

expectations of man, for this would be to provide a yardstick "from below" for measuring what the historic revelation might contain and so limit in advance the divine generosity. For Balthasar, it is not so much the *subjective* as the *objective* conditions of possibility for a revelation that ought to be the *primary* concern of the theologian. And the latter show the glory of God streaming out through the revelatory form in a way which it has not entered the heart of man to imagine, much less to anticipate. It is the categorial object of Jesus's (divinely personalised) humanity which *is* the transcendent theophany, for the light of God breaks out from within the concrete form and does not merely fall upon it. Moreover, in Balthasar's theology of the perpetual renewal of the revelation once given, the disciples are called to be themselves mediating forms – realities which continue to present to us the saving presence of Christ, a notion of vocation (and so, again, of mission) hard to re-cast into the terms of a transcendental anthropology of finite and infinite spirit.

But for Balthasar – and here we return once more to pastoral considerations – it is precisely in a humanistic age that one should *not* introduce into Catholic theology an "anthropological turn", for this would almost certainly subject revelation, in such a cultural context, to the domination of an anthropological system. Whether Rahner, with his mystagogical emphasis on man before the mystery of God, has himself fallen into that easy trap, is another question. In his own words (which might just as easily be Balthasar's):

> God remains God, the first and ultimate measure which can be measured by nothing else... the mystery who alone is self evident... the Holy One who is really only accessible in worship.[24]

And Balthasar too, after all, describes Christ as the concrete norm not only for ontology but also for anthropology, just as Rahner defines anthropology as deficient Christology. But Balthasar would comment, I think, that in the context of his own theology, entranced by the glory of God in the aesthetics, challenged by the

---

[24] *Foundations of Christian Faith*, op. cit., pp. 119-120.

substitutionary redemptive initiative of God in the dramatics, and commited to the working out of a specifically Christological grammar for the "speech" of God in the logic, such a statement could not be abused in the way that Rahner's thought unfortunately has been. As with much of the *nouvelle théologie* inheritance from the 1950's, what was once meant to sacralise the secular (namely, the elision, except at the most formal level, of the distinction between natural and supernatural) has now come to secularise the sacred – for the sake, as many would say, of applying the Church's teaching to the "contemporary faith-situation" in a "pastorally meaningful way". But as Balthasar remarked in an interview barely a decade after the Second Vatican Council's ending:

> The Church reflects too little on the treasure in the field. She has sold much. But has she really got the treasure in return?[25]

How the treasure – the Kingdom – comes to Christians is through faith in the atoning work of the Incarnate One, as expressed sacramentally, ascetically, mystically and missiologically in the life of the Church at its most intense, for, as Origen says, Christ is *autobasileia*, the Kingdom itself. How it comes to non-Christians remains unknown.

While Rahner and Balthasar cannot be made to agree on the topic of anonymous Christianity, were we, in conclusion, to seek for a way in which their wider theological approaches might be regarded as complementary and not simply in competition, this would have to be along the lines of their adopting respectively a subject-oriented (Rahner) and an object-oriented (Balthasar) approach to the same saving revelation. This point has been put persuasively by Archbishop Rowan Williams, who writes that, while Rahner's Christ is an answer to the human question, Balthasar's is a question to all human answers.[26] In Jeffrey Kay's summing up of Balthasar's theological method in this connexion:

---

[25] "Geist und Feuer", *Herder Korrespondenz* 30 (1976), p. 78.

[26] R. D. Williams, "Balthasar and Rahner", in J. Riches (ed.), *The Analogy of Beauty: The Theology of Hans Urs von Balthasar* (Edinburgh 1986), p. 34.

> The form of Christ makes a new revelation with its own evidence which no insight into human dynamism can anticipate or verify. Christian faith is based radically on the a posteriori evidence of Christ's historical form and not primarily on ahistorical, a priori evidence that has been awakened or mediated to itself on the occasion of a posteriori experience.[27]

And yet Balthasar can also, like Rahner, speak of the need for a "pre-understanding" of what is given in the form of historical revelation: central thereto, in his exposition in *Herrlichkeit*, are the analogically-related experiences of inter-personal love and art, since in each of these cases we have to do with the perception of something unique. The human being naturally pursues the transcendent – there *is* a religious a priori ordered to revelation, and it is, furthermore, transformed by the grace God offers humankind into what Balthasar calls a theological a priori as well.[28] And yet – here we have the characteristic difference of emphasis from Rahner – these existentials are *ordered to* the objective, a posteriori vision of Jesus's form, the concrete theophany celebrated at Christmas and Easter, for which the experience of uniqueness in love and art prepare us. They are *for* the *Transzendenzgestalt* of the Incarnate Image, and not simply ("real-symbolically") effected by the same. But Rahner too would agree that the "blessed Mystery" into which, on his account, the combination of transcendental and categorical revelation draws the human subject cannot be "seen" except by reference to the unique embodied humanity of the Saviour, which remains in heaven of abiding decisive significance for our salvation.[29]

---

[27] "Aesthetics and a posteriori evidence in Balthasar's Theological Method", *Communio*, Winter 1975, p. 191.

[28] *The Glory of the Lord: A Theological Aesthetics: I. Seeing the Form* (Et Edinburgh 1982), p. 167.

[29] "The Eternal Significance of the Humanity of Jesus for our Relationship with God", in *Theological Investigations* III (Et London 1967), pp. 35-46.

VII

CARDINAL RATZINGER ON THEOLOGY, LITURGY, FAITH

Cardinal Joseph Ratzinger is hardly an unknown name to those who follow the current affairs of the Catholic Church. His well-publicised interventions in regard either to entire movements of theological and moral thought or vis-à-vis such individual writers as the Sri Lankan theologian Tissa Balasuriya have gained him nicknames like *Panzerkardinal* and "Grand Inquisitor", and if the latter is scarcely original and the former may betray a phobia about Germany and the will to power, these titles make up in ubiquity for whatever they lack in wit. In Michael O'Brien's novel *Father Elijah*, an apocalyptic account of the possible coming state of things, one of the characters, an English priest in the Curia, calls "Dottrina" – a lightly fictionalized Ratzinger – "probably the most unpopular man in the world". Should he read O'Brien's novel, I doubt that the cardinal would be unduly distressed, given his own words:

> When the bearers of the apostolic office dare today to exercise the authority which has been committed to them in matters of doctrine, they enter almost invariably into the form of apostolic existence depicted by St Paul, "We have become and are now as the refuse of the world, the offscourings of all things"(I Corinthians 4, 17). The authority of the Church can continue to be exercised in our society only under the sign of contradiction and precisely in this way it returns to its true nature.[1]

In reality, of course, O'Brien is employing hyperbole, legitimised from a literary standpoint by the need to underline his theme of confrontation become crisis – though some knowledge of

---

[1] J. Ratzinger, *The Nature and Mission of Theology: Approaches to Understanding its Role in the Light of Present Contoversy* (San Francisco 1995), pp. 7-8.

biographical facts emerges when O'Brien's Mgr. William Stansgby comments

> He's without guile, as clear as a bell. He hates *romanità* with a passion and never uses it.[2]

One of the ways in which Ratzinger's *modus operandi* differs from that of Curial cardinals as a species consists in his willingness and even eagerness, to produce and publish personal analyses of the state of the Church – the condition of her religious, pastoral, intellectual, moral, liturgical and (so far as it still exists) artistic culture. Such analyses are distinct from but, evidently, not unrelated to the official documents of his dicastery, the Congregation for the Doctrine of the Faith. They are distinct from the documents in *genre* since they take the form of books published by commercial presses or articles in learned journals or interviews with journalists and publicists, and no Curialist could by any stretch of the imagination regard such media as possible means for the authoritative promulgation of the teaching of the Roman magisterium. Yet these analyses must be related to Ratzinger's work, precisely as Prefect of his Congregation – as, that is, papal vicar for doctrine in the universal Church – because the self-same judgment is operating in these two modalities.

Can we get an – at any rate, partial – overview of the way that in the last ten years (in the period since I wrote a survey of his theology published in 1988) Cardinal Ratzinger's mind has been moving as it surveys the state of the Catholic Church, its thought, worship and prospects in the years of the millennium's close?[3]

Before grappling with particular issues, it may be helpful to get some idea of the lines on which, according to Ratzinger, the Church's intellectual life should be running. Especially useful for this purpose is the essay collection *Wesen und Auftrag der Theologie* (1993) from whose English translation I have already quoted. The

---

[2] M. D. O'Brien, *Father Elijah, An Apocalypse* (Et San Francisco 1996), p. 72.

[3] A. Nichols, O. P., *The Theology of Joseph Ratzinger: An Introductory Study* (Edinburgh 1988). The present essay was written too early to take into account Ratzinger's most recent, and serene, theology of worship in *Der Geist der Liturgie: Eine Einführung* (Freiburg im Breisgau 2000).

book's preface states in unmistakable terms the key issue as Ratzinger sees it. That is, we discover, the coherence of Catholicism as an historically defined revelation-borne totality of faith and practice. Where the world still has expectations of theologians, such expectations, Ratzinger suggests, usually turn out to be fourfold. First, by the critical use of reason, the theologian is supposed to determine what in Christianity is still worth preserving, setting boundaries thereby to the *de facto* Church. Secondly, the theologian is also expected to offer orientation in the human need for transcendence and spirituality. Thirdly, he or she must promote dialogue between world religions, and support whatever practical proposals there may be to further the unification of the planet, as conveniently summed up in the World Council of Churches mission-statement: "justice, peace and the integrity of creation". Finally, the theologian is also supposed to be a doctor of souls, helping individuals to accept their own personalities positively, striving to overcome factors that make for alienation. This quartet of imperatives – rational, spiritual, political and psychological – at least in their contemporary form, derive more from the history of culture than from the Church's definition of the Gospel. So it is not surprising if they place the theologians who treat them as suitable marching orders in a certain situation of tension with a more classical account of what theology is all about.[4] And when she turns her mind to the subject, that

---

[4] As Hans Urs von Balthasar told the still youthful (and theologically a touch or two less solid) Ratzinger in the immediately post-Conciliar period, "Do not presuppose the faith but propose it!" This, for Ratzinger, is the genesis of the *Catechism of the Catholic Church*:

"The bishops present at the 1985 Synod called for a universal catechism of the whole Church because they sensed precisely what Balthasar had put into words in his note to me. Their experience as shepherds had shown them that the various new pastoral activities have no solid basis unless they are irradiations and applications of the message of faith. Faith cannot be presupposed; it must be proposed. This is the purpose of the *Catechism*. It aims to propose the faith in its fullness and wealth, but also in its unity and simplicity". [J. Ratzinger, *Gospel, Catechesis, Catechism: Sidelights on the "Catechism of the Catholic Church"* (San Francisco 1995), p. 24.]

more classical account (my terminology, not his) is that of the Church herself in her doctrinal capacity. As Ratzinger puts it:

> While the theologian is busily working to meet these expectations, the institutional Church often appears to be an annoying impediment. This is especially true of the magisterium of the Catholic Church, which presupposes that Christianity, especially in its Catholic variety, has a determinate content and thus confronts our thinking with a prior given, which cannot be manipulated at will and which alone gives to the theologian's words their distinctive significance above and beyond all purely political or philosophical discourse. To do theology – as the magisterium understands theology – it is not sufficient merely to calculate how much religion can reasonably be expected of man and to utilize bits and pieces of the Christian tradition accordingly. Theology is born when the arbitrating judgment of reason encounters a limit, in that we discover something which we have not excogitated ourselves but which has been revealed to us. For this reason, not every religious theory has the right to label itself as Christian or Catholic theology simply because it wishes to do so; whoever would lay claim to this title is obliged to accept as meaningful the prior given which goes along with it.[5]

A fuller recovery of the essentially ecclesial character of Catholic thought would have the desirable side-effect, moreover, of inhibiting any further development of that unhelpful know-nothingism where the baptised intellect, alarmed by the alliance of popular theologians with the *Zeitgeist*, flees from its responsibility to the things of the mind, its duty (in the words of First Peter) to "give a reason for the hope that is in [it]" (3, 15).

The controversies aroused by Ratzinger's doctrinal interventions may seem divisive, but, he implies, the only internal unity worth having in the Catholic Church is not a unity based on mere consensus, much less one created by the agreement of the various interested parties to differ, but, rather, a unity founded on authentic understanding of the truth of revelation itself. It is this concern for clarity in the service of objective coherence, as much as

---

[5] J. Ratzinger, *The Nature and Mission of Theology*, op. cit., pp. 7-8.

any particular conclusion at which he may arrive, that makes Ratzinger unpopular with that (fortunately, still small) portion of the episcopate for whom opinion polls and media comment count as important if not decisive factors in framing the pastoral government of the Church.

I pass now, after these general remarks, to Ratzinger's analyses of particular problems, issues, areas, but I will return to touch (briefly) on his overall picture of the theologian-in-the Church once again at the end.

The topic with which Ratzinger's name is most famously linked is *liberation theology*. At the beginning of the period which this presentation is meant to cover, Ratzinger made a substantial analysis of the issues involved in a lecture to the Rhineland Westphalia Academy of Sciences under the title "Politics and Redemption: The Relation of Faith, Rationality and the Irrational in the so-called Theology of Liberation".[6] Ratzinger did not deny that the problem identified by liberation theology – how to relate redemption to situations of manifest and seemingly hopeless poverty, powerlessness and absence of justice – was, in his own words, "not only justified but necessary". Not the *Ausgangspunkt*, the departure point, but the *Lösungsvorschlag*, the solution proposed, is what he contested. Would that proposal lead, he asked, to a politics that were both inherently sound and also theologically redemptive – meaning, in the case of the latter phrase, able to fill with real substance the doctrines which the theological patrimony contains? Perhaps to our surprise, Ratzinger's initial criticism, which is focussed on the Peruvian theologian Gustavo Gutiérrez's *Teología de la Liberación*, is not concerned so much with orthodoxy of doctrine as with the political and theological irrationality in which, he believes, that flag-ship of the liberation theology movement was foundering. For on the political level, while, he thought, Gutiérrez had rightly drawn attention to the anthropological feebleness and unilaterally

---

[6] J. Ratzinger "Politik und Erlösung: Zum Verhältnis von Glaube, Rationalität und Irrationalem in der sogenannten Theologie der Befreiung", = *Rhenisch Westfälische Akademie der Wissenschaften, Vorträge* G279 (Opladen 1986).

quantitative character of the once fashionable "developmental" theories of Third World social economies (since when considered as general accounts of what constitutes human flourishing these were remarkably weak), the book simply did not provide the argumentation necessary to convince the reader that a combined diet of Fidel Castro, Camilo Torres and Che Guevara, supplemented by a cocktail of references to Marx, Freud and the "New Left" sociologist Herbert Marcuse, furnished a credible answer to the question thus raised. As Ratzinger writes:

> How is the mounting of a social revolution for the sake of a cultural revolution to lead to a new human being? What forces are going to mould him? What sort of freedom is it that such liberation gives him? Doesn't the humanistic goal here have to cover up the holes in the political and economic argument, just as, conversely, political pragmatism will have to close the yawning gap in anthropology?[7]

The deficit which Gutiérrez's account showed in terms of political and economic credibility increased staggeringly, Ratzinger continued, when his book was assessed in terms of its theological consistency and credibility. Whereas the progressive majority at the Second Vatican Council wished, over against the conservative minority, to relativise the distinction between the natural and the supernatural orders, insisting that the distinction has its place only *within* the single saving plan of God for the world, Gutiérrez considers that nothing short of the fullscale obliteration of that distinction will do. While such representatives of the conciliar majority as the German Cardinals Döpfner and Frings, Ratzinger's patron at Vatican II, considered the nature-supernature distinction, albeit relativised, nonetheless vital if the corresponding distinction between the world and the Church was to continue to be maintained, Gutiérrez opined that for this very reason it had to go. Human progress cannot be understood as something distinct from redemption, save formally speaking – that is, as a pure concept. As Ratzinger summarises the thought of the father of liberation theology on this point:

---

[7] Ibid., pp. 11-12.

> The temple of God in this world is... history. The movement
> from Old to New Testaments is not a spiritualisation but a
> materialisation. That whereas God's little temple is the
> community, his great temple is history, signifies the way
> encounter with God takes place in history to the extent that
> people commit themselves to the historical becoming of
> humankind.[8]

But though the material referents of the concepts of human
progress on the one hand, and redemption on the other, in this
way coincide, that is so, Gutiérrez explains, only with regard to the
central core of such referring. Actually, the Kingdom of God is
more than any form of social order no matter how emancipated –
and here he could cite the Jewish thinker Ernst Bloch in whose
secularised eschatology the ground of human hope lies in what
Bloch called "the being of the not yet", to which by definition
there is no end. Ratzinger's fundamental theological – as distinct
from political – objection to *Teología de la Liberación* does not lie,
therefore, in the claim that here the distinction between natural
and supernatural is elided because, even on Gutiérrez's view, some
task remains for a meta-sociology to perform and thus a version of
the idea of the gratuity of grace is retained. Rather is his
theological objection that Gutiérrez, by fusing theological reason
with political from the outset, can point to no significant content
for this further task – talk of which thus becomes a kind of pious
ornament lacking all real relation to the substance of his discourse.
For Gutiérrez, the proper object of a faith that transcends the
humanistic aspirations of a future-oriented social project is the
forgiveness of sins, considered as making possible a common
lifestyle with God and with other men and women. But this has
no genuine rôle to play in his whole scheme. If, on the one hand,
the medium of encounter with God (life with God) is the
emancipatory process itself and, on the other, the immanent goal
of the Utopian politics he recommends is already the full creation
of human community (life with other people), Gutiérrez may
distinguish between social Utopia as man's achievement and the

---

[8]Ibid., p. 14.

Gospel promises as the direct gift of God but what the latter adds to the former remains quite unclear in his thought. Ratzinger, therefore, ends his analysis of Gutiérrez's work with the comment:

> There is no reason to doubt the seriousness with which this proviso in favour of orthodoxy is entered in Gutiérrez. But what is equally clear is the lack of any function which this affirmation can serve. Similarly, the total subordination of all empirical analysis and political reflection to the historical project of Utopia-making lies open for all to see. Insofar as rationality and faith are brought into play at all, both of them are placed at the service of Utopia, itself the power which is to mobilise and gather into one humanity as a whole.[9]

It is only fair to add that subsequently Ratzinger would cite Gutiérrez as the model of a truly humble and therefore impressive theologian for his willingness to think through again some of these connexions, or the lack of them, in the light of the criticism of his work made by the Peruvian bishops and, insofar as it belongs with the wider corpus of liberation theology, by the two critiques, negative and positive, of the Holy See.

Speaking to the combined episcopates of Latin America a decade later, in 1996, Ratzinger registered the collapse in the meanwhile of the European Marxist-Leninist State systems, and the consequent discrediting of Marxism as a philosophy of socially transformative action. But, he observed, simply to adopt an attitude of gleeful satisfaction at this turn of an historical corner would be, for the Church, short-sighted and unwise. For in the first place the non-fulfilment of the Marxian hope for a systematically better future has left a void of disillusion which no other force has as yet been able to fill. In the absence of agreement as to the scope of the concept of justice and effective means to translate idea into reality, new versions of the Marxist hope are quite likely to revive in the world of the future.

More immediately, however, the chief consequence of the quasi-disappearance, or at least occlusion, of Marxism is to reinforce an already potent tendency in the non-Marxist West

---

[9] Ibid., p. 17.

towards a thorough-going relativism as the prevailing philosophical *Weltanschauung* of our time. As he told the bishops:

> Marxism believed it knew the structure of world history and, from there, it tried to show how history could be led definitively along the right path... The failure of the only scientifically based system for solving human problems could well be taken only to justify nihilism or, at any rate, total relativism.[10]

The *relativism* which Ratzinger believes now to have replaced Marxism as the chief threat to the Church's faith is in the first place a European (and by extension North American) phenomenon. It is, as he puts it, "Europe's post-metaphysical philosophy". Such relativism is not defined only negatively, as the resignedness of the enquiring mind before the immensity of a total truth too great for man to master. Relativism is also defined positively (and herein lies its imperialistic character) as a necessary pre-condition for the flourishing of tolerance, freedom, and, in the political sphere, democracy. All these concepts and their attendant practices would be imperilled, it is said, if people were to affirm the existence of a single truth valid for all. Ratzinger concedes that, were the moral absolutes to be acknowledged (but in a society which, for instance, claims the "right" to take unborn life, this is already a very big "if"), no harm is done when political society is built up on the basis that "all roads are mutually recognised as fragments of the effort toward that which is better". Indeed, the refusal to grant at least a degree of such pluralism in the matter of means was a typical folly of the Marxist State. The danger to the Church arises from the extension of such relativism to the realms of ethics and religion. Ratzinger deplores the fact that the pluralist theology of religions of the English Presbyterian John Hick has gained converts among Catholic writers on inter-faith dialogue, singling out for particular attention the American Paul Knitter,

---

[10] J. Ratzinger, "Current Situation of Faith and Theology", *Osservatore Romano* (English language edition), 45. 6 (November 1996), p. 4.

author of *No Other Name*.[11] Knitter's philosophical mentor, writing within a Kantian framework for which ultimate reality is not available to us since we know only "appearances", abandoned, after a spell (significantly) in India a previous attempt at a Christ-centred theology of religions in favour of one which would be theo- but not Christo-logical.[12] Ratzinger describes the result as follows:

> Jesus is consciously relativized as one religious leader among others. The Absolute cannot come into history, only models and ideal forms that remind us about what within history can never as such be grasped. And so concepts like the Church, dogma, the sacraments, must lose their unconditional character. To absolutise such limited forms of mediation or, worse still, to consider them as real encounters with the universally valid truth of the self-revealing God, would be equivalent to elevating oneself to the category of the Absolute, thereby losing the infiniteness of the totally other God.

To ascribe to the figure of Jesus Christ, or the faith of his Church, a universal, binding truth, valid for all generations, cultures, individuals, is, on this view, mere fundamentalism, and as such subversive of the basic good of modernity itself, namely, tolerance in freedom. Giving unique status to Jesus Christ and, in dependence on him, to his Church, generates a tribalism and ultimately a fanaticism which snaps the bond linking religious faith to brotherly (and sisterly) love. Dialogue, therefore, must be radically re-conceived no longer as the most respectful form of testimony in mission but as mission's antithesis. As Ratzinger concludes:

> The relativist dissolution of Christology and even more of ecclesiology thus becomes a central commandment of religion.[13]

Such a relativist theology of religions has, Ratzinger continues, a special appeal in the Indian sub-continent, owing to the

---

[11] P.J. Knitter, *No Other Name: A Critical Survey of Christian Attitudes* toward the World Religions (New York 1995).

[12] J. Hick, *God and the Universe of Faiths* (London 1977; 1990).

[13] J. Ratzinger, "Current Situation of Faith and Theology", art. cit., p. 4

unexpected family resemblance between the post-metaphysical European mind and the traditional negative theology of India. The essential relativism of all religious forms vis-à-vis Brahman, the Absolute of Hindu philosophy, has long been a datum of the Indian inheritance. In the Indian context it seems especially natural to set aside the centrality of the image of Christ, and instead to classify Jesus as one more saviour figure of history, one manifestation of the saving power of the Logos (to return to the language of Scripture) rather than the Logos himself. And in the framework of the meeting of East and West, the global dialogue of religions, relativism appears accordingly as the true if belatedly (re-) discovered philosophy of humanity itself.

What, concretely, then, is the follower of such a revised, self-consciously relativistic Christianity to do? In *An Interpretation of Religion: Human Response to the Transcendent*[14], Hick enters an appeal that we become more "reality-centred" on the grounds that, if generalised, this would amount to a movement of convergence on the part of (potentially) all followers of all religions. Unfortunately, as Ratzinger points out, the imperative "be reality-centred" is largely vacuous. Like Martin Heidegger's call to "be authentic" which so influenced the exegetical star of modern Protestant liberalism Rudolf Bultmann, it may mean anything or nothing according to choice. And this, so Ratzinger thinks, is why we are now seeing a definite tendency to "overcome the void of a theory of religion reduced to the categorical imperative" by the forging of a link between pluralist religion on the one side and a revived liberation theology on the other. Inter-religious dialogue is to become ideationally manageable through conceptual simplification and at the same time of some effect in practice by the reinstatement of liberation theology's watchword: orthopraxy before orthodoxy.

And this is precisely the mixture of ingredients to be found in the work of the Sri Lankan theologian, excommunicated in January 1997, Tissa Balasuriya. A writer hardly known outside the

---

[14] J. Hick, *An Interpretation of Religion: Human Response to the Transcendent* (New Haven 1989).

Third World and in no sense an academic theologian was considered a menace owing to the hopes the Catholic Church has invested in Asian evangelization in the third millennium.[15]

However, as Ratzinger commented to the bishops of Latin America, if "orthopraxy" in this inter-religious context is understood in a socio-political fashion, as with early liberation theology, then the criteria for what should count as "correct" action become quite unclear – unless, that is, over against the magisterium, one were to re-impose a Marxist understanding of praxis, logical and consistent as that is within its own terms. Moreover, were such "orthopraxy" to be understood, rather, in terms of ethics, then the impossibility of commending a substantive morality on the basis of relativist presuppositions would soon empty it of content. There is left, if we are to give any sense to the term, only, in the context of Catholic-Hindu dialogue, the notion of orthopraxy as *cultic* practice – exploration of which, Ratzinger thinks, would genuinely repay inter-faith investigation, as well as having clear affinities with the notion of *orthodoxy*, since, as the etymology of that word indicates, the original meaning of being orthodox was precisely to "know and practise the right way in which God wants to be glorified".[16]

What, though, leaving Asia, are the telltale signs of the spread of religious relativism in the *Western* world? Ratzinger locates the fruits of such relativism in two very different places – in the rise of, first of all, that disparate yet influential movement "New Age", but also, secondly, and by sharp contrast, the intensification of what he terms "pragmatism" in Church life with its familiar effects, for Western Catholics, in matters both pastoral and liturgical. For the supporters of New Age, so Ratzinger writes:

> the solution to the problem of relativity must not be sought in
> a new encounter of the self with another, or others, but by

---

[15] R. Moynihan, "Does the Thunder Presage a Storm?", *Inside the Vatican* (February 1997), p.16

[16] J. Ratzinger, "Current Situation of Faith and Theology", art. cit., p. 5.

overcoming the subject, in an ecstatic return to the cosmic dance.[17]

If there is no commonly available truth, then Christianity can be set aside in favour of "the re-editing of pre-Christian religions and cultures", all ordered to maximalising the possible ways of experiencing the Absolute by way of a new gnosis which, like the Gnosticism faced by the Ancient Church, presses into its service a variety of ill-assorted fragments of contemporary science – biology, psychology, physics. As God withdraws from the space of Western society, the gods return, offering to let us "perceive for a moment the pleasure of the infinite and forget the misery of the finite". And that is very much the temptation to its Western converts, so Ratzinger believes, of Buddhism – hence the perhaps unfortunate reference to "spiritual auto-eroticism" in his interview with the French *journal d'actualité L'Express* in March 1997.[18]

It may seem a far cry from New Age and Western Buddhism to pastoral pragmatism, appeals for democratization in Church government and liturgical horizontalism, but Ratzinger has reason to think that all these phenomena are interconnected. For once again, unless the faith and the apostolic ministry of the Church come to us through the Word incarnate and the Church he founded, they possess no unconditional value – so why not treat Catholicism in a purely pragmatic way? If relativism in the fashion of the Catholic disciples of Hick is correct, then the faith is something about which we ourselves may decide. In such a context, what does not command a majority vote in the opinion polls can hardly be obligatory, though by the same token a majority can scarcely impose its view on a minority either. In any case, a faith whose content is determined after the fashion of a party programme, rather than by appeal to the Church of all ages, is not the Catholic faith as hitherto known.

So far as *the Liturgy* is concerned, much the same pragmatic mind-set is at work. The post-conciliar liturgical reform of the Roman rite in its various phases unintentionally introduced the

---

[17] Ibid.
[18] "Le Testament du Panzerkardinal", *L'Express*, 20 March 1997, p. 70.

idea that Liturgy is something patent of endless reconstruction, according to taste. And if a central authority in Rome can do this, then why cannot a local authority, in a particular diocese, and if a particular or diocesan church can do it, then why not one parish within that church, or one group within that parish? This is an issue to which Ratzinger has devoted much attention as bears witness the 1995 essay collection *Ein neues Lied für den Herren*.[19] The book's sub-title "Faith in Christ and Liturgy in the Present Age", already suggests how he links the fate of the Liturgy, like that of a relativism-imperilled theology, to fluctuations in the understanding of the person of Christ.

According to Ratzinger, the criteria for liturgical renewal are inseparable from the question posed by Jesus to his disciples at Caesarea Philippi, "Who do you say that the Son of Man is" (Matthew 16, 13, and parallels). Thus, for example, if we credit the claim that, as human beings ourselves, we can meaningfully follow only the prophetic lead of the man Jesus whereas the divine Christ lacks existential relevance for us, then the trajectory of discipleship will inevitably fall short of its true goal – entry into the divine life – and this cannot fail to have its effect on our liturgical theory and practice. The hope for liberation through the Gospel becomes *kitschig und kleinig*, (kitschy and homey), rather than aiming at the heights where the Son made man, having made satisfaction for our sins, sits at the right hand of the Father.[20]

Ratzinger considers that, viewed historically, the deficient Christology which he takes as a key to an aesthetically impoverished liturgical horizontalism derives from certain flaws in the inter-War movement of *ressourcement* with whose main lines he is in other respects fully identified. One shared theme of the biblical and liturgical movements of those years when the theology that made the Council was gestating, was a renewed emphasis on the humanity of Christ. One finds it in doctrinal theology in, for instance, the Tübingen theologian Karl Adam's *Christus unser*

---

[19] J. Ratzinger, *Ein neues Lied für den Herren: Christusglaube und Liturgie der Gegenwart* (Freiburg 1995).
[20] Ibid., p. 19.

Bruder[21]. One finds it also in liturgiological mode in the claim of the Innsbruck liturgist Josef Jungmann that the Church, during her struggle against the Arianism which reduced Christ to a creature, albeit the most excellent one, relaxed her guard against an opposite danger, a quasi-Monophysitism invading the Liturgy where it left its mark in the introduction of prayers directed not to the Father but to the Son, and infecting via the Liturgy the piety of the faithful: thus Jungmann's *Die Stellung Christi im liturgischen Gebet*.[22] In Ratzinger's view both projects (Adam's and Jungmann's) unwittingly affected the Liturgy to adverse effect by insinuating a humanistic Christ no longer capable of inserting the temporal into the eternal in his own person.

But as biblical scholarship moves on it discovers that the attempt to describe the humanity of Jesus without the incarnational narrative or to locate a Jesus of history without the full biblical portrait of the Christ produces distinctly nugatory results. As historical enquiry into the origins and development of the Liturgy advances, it finds public invocation of the Saviour before the watershed of the Council of Nicaea. And as patristic erudition accumulates, scholars have realised the decisive importance of the work of Maximus the Confessor and the Third Council of Constantinople which canonised his achievement in its teaching that in the person of the Word incarnate two freedoms, one divine, the other human, are perfectly synthesized, so that the possibility of following Jesus' human will while bracketing his divine does not arise. All these are examples, evidently, of where Ratzinger sees scholarly advance patently *assisting* the Church's continuing appropriation of her own faith.

The Letter to the Hebrews called Christ "the same yesterday, today and for ever" (13, 80) and we cannot meet him, accordingly, save in all three dimensions together. Since one of those dimensions is eternal, relationship with Christ is bungled if

---

[21]K. Adam, *Christus unser Bruder* (Regensburg 1926; 1930[2]); Et *Christ our Brother* (New York 1931).

[22] J. Jungmann, *Die Stellung Christi im liturgischen Gebet* (Münster 1925; 1962[2]); Et *The Place of Christ in Liturgical Prayer* (London 1965).

143

we fail to step over the threshold of the temporal into that which is time's origin and goal. A liturgical culture centred on a Jesus presented chiefly as the champion of a freer spirituality, a more broadminded morality, or an improved political structure can only be, by contrast, a moralising affair, from which the glory has departed that once led through the Paschal mystery to the heavenly places. Moreover, owing to attenuation of the idea of guilt (except in the pathological form in which guilt belongs on the psychiatric couch), the Christian doctrine of redemption can barely now be grasped. Ideas of expiation, supplication and reparatory satisfaction central to the Atonement and so to the sacrifice of the altar, the mid-point of the entire Liturgy, say nothing to the contemporary West. Hence, once again, the success of Christ the political liberator or the psychic healer – a reference to the much-read work of the priest-psychiatrist Eugen Drewermann. In both schemes, the one collective, the other individual, redemption becomes auto-liberation by reference to Jesus as human model, and the Church and her worship lose their salvific meaning. The Liturgy's aim gets re-defined as the constitution and experience of community as such, something only too welcome in an atomised society thirsting for sociality, and the beauty of the Liturgy malforms more than ever did the much-maligned cultus of the Baroque into a spiritual show where the showmaster-president is concerned above all to make religion interesting, whereas what the Liturgy should mediate is encounter with the living God who dwarfs all humanly initiated action.[23]

Not that the truncation of liturgical consciousness can be attributed exclusively to a reduced Christology. The trivialization of the Liturgy would have been hard enough to prevent, Ratzinger surmises, in a world where the existence of God is deemed irrelevant to the shaping of human life, and the very question as to what can be known shrinks to the this-worldly proportions of Kant's *phainomenon*. Without a metaphysical renaissance,

---

[23] For an overview of Ratzinger's liturgical theology, see D. Sureau, "La Liturgie sans Eglise: La crise de la liturgie selon le cardinal Ratzinger", *Sedes Sapientiae* 56 (1996), pp. 1-17.

considers Ratzinger, the God of Judaeo-Christianity will become in the West, like the high gods of many polytheisms in the past, a *deus otiosus*, retreating to such remoteness as to be superfluous. There needs to be a renewal of metaphysics because without ontology the question of God cannot rationally be raised: after all, it is none other than the question of the origin and goal of reality as a whole. On this there stands or falls, says Ratzinger, the continued existence of the Church's missionary endeavour when the latter is considered as the spreading of a truth destined for all people.

> The universality of faith, which is a basic presupposition of the missionary task, is both meaningful and morally defensible only if this faith really is oriented beyond the symbolism of the religions toward an answer meant for all, an answer which also appeals to the common reason of mankind.[24]

In his essay "Ways of Faith in the Breakthrough of the Present", one of several studies which pose the question, Are we at a turning-point for Europe?[25], Ratzinger argues that it was the narrowing down of that concept of rationality by the eighteenth century Enlightenment which, by reaction, opened the door to the various irrational ideologies – Romantic and post-Romantic – of the modern world. It will be, he predicts, through a recovery of the Johannine insight, "In the beginning was the Word" (John 1: 1), that reason and faith will simultaneously be re-installed in the West, for the "logos" which was in the beginning is the creative reason of God himself, a creative reason revealed through its embodiment in Jesus Christ to be also love, and revealed, furthermore, in the sending of his Spirit by the glorified Lord to be no inefficacious love, love as sentiment, but rather love as power.

---

[24]J. Ratzinger, *The Nature and Mission of Theology*, op. cit., p. 25.   In this section I have drawn on material expounded more fully in A. Nichols, O. P., "Zion and Philistia: the Liturgy and Theological Aesthetics Today", *Downside Review* 115. 398 (1997), pp. 53-73.

[25] J. Ratzinger, *Ein Wendezeit für Europa? Diagnosen und Prognosen zur Lage von Kirche und Welt* (Einsiedeln-Freiburg 1991), pp. 75-76.

Thus, on Ratzinger's view, the rediscovery of Christian orthodoxy will restore to the West not only its heart but also its *intelligence* as well. That is for him the deepest reason why the magisterium and the University theologian cannot in the last analysis be counter-posed. And not only heart and intelligence are involved. So also is moral performance, since, as Ratzinger remarks in his *Salz der Erde*, a book of conversations with the German publicist Peter Seewald, in a society where the highest court of appeal is "public opinion and its judgments", the motivating power of ethical ideals in the lives of individuals may often be "very slight".[26]

The student of Christian origins and celebrated apostate Ernest Renan once remarked that only when the Church lost the will to maintain the Inquisition did she cease to be a key factor in the fortunes of Western culture. I cannot imagine that Cardinal Ratzinger would wish to restore the civil-legal position of his Congregation, yet his ability not only to analyse the state of things by reference to evangelical criteria (and it is this critical rôle I have stressed here), but also to project re-construction would qualify him for the post of minister for culture in any predominantly Christian society. The passionate intellectuality, taking the special form of a gift to show where ideas tend, is more comparable to such German intellectuals arrived on Anglo-Saxon shores as Sir Isaiah Berlin and Hannah Arendt than of the "general officers" once responsible for *Blitzkrieg*. Though in the early years of John Paul II's pontificate it became a cliché to describe Ratzinger as "poacher turned gamekeeper", the erstwhile reformer now become restorationist conserver (of course the justice of that description turns on what one thinks the Second Vatican Council set out to do in the first place), I prefer to an agricultural a horticultural metaphor. To a gardener, tending plants and pruning them often amount to the same thing, and not least when a garden is – like modern Catholicism, vital but rank – in the eloquent Cockney idiom "blooming awful".

---

[26] J. Ratzinger, *Salz der Erde: Christentum und katholische Kirche an der Jahrtausendwende: Ein Gespräch mit Peter Seewald* (Stuttgart 1996), p. 157.

PART TWO

LITURGY

VIII

ODO CASEL REVISITED

Johannes Casel was born on 27 September 1886 in the neighbourhood of Koblenz, the historic city at the confluence of the Rhine and the Moselle (hence its name, *Confluentes*, of which "Koblenz" is a corruption). The "principal seat of the Rhenish wine-trade", as the eleventh edition of *Encyclopaedia Britannica* described it on the eve of the Great War, the town of Casel's boyhood and teenage years was also a manufactory of mineral waters as well as pianos and paper, machinery, boats and barges.[1] Johannes was not, we can suppose, drawn by any of these but by the clamant Catholicism of the city, scene of important synods of the Frankish church toward the end of the first millennium, until in 1018 the emperor Henry II transferred it outright to the care of the archbishop of Trier. It would remain under the latter's jurisdiction, civil and ecclesiastical, until the Revolutionary armies – goaded beyond endurance by the welcome that prelate, latterly resident there, gave the emigrés fleeing from M. Guillotin's invention – seized Koblenz in 1794, less than a century before Casel's birth. After twenty years of French rule, the Congress of Vienna awarded it to Prussia. Though the great Austrian statesman, Metternich, had been born there in 1773, and the palace of the princes Metternich was situated in the Neustadt or Klemensstadt (named after the last archbishop-elector Clemens Wenceslaus who did much to adorn it), and that connexion, between Vienna and the episcopal statelet on the rivers of the far West, testifies to the political flexibility of the old multijurisdictional, pre-Revolutionary German Reich, the day of archbishop-electors was irremediably past. Some few miles down the Rhine from Koblenz another Henry II – not, this time, the

---

[1] "Coblenz", *The Encyclopaedia Britannica: A Dictionary of Arts, Sciences, Literature and General Information*, VI (Cambridge 1910), p. 612.

emperor, but the Count Palatine of that name and number – had, with his wife, founded in 1093 the abbey of Maria Laach, St. Mary of the Lake. At the time of Casel's birth, its magnificent Romanesque church was almost entirely intact. Though suppressed and secularized during the Revolution, the monastic buildings had returned to Church hands when the Society of Jesus bought them in 1862, and made of Maria Laach a major study centre, home to the influential Jesuit periodical *Stimmen der Zeit,* which began life, in fact, under the name *Stimmen aus Maria Laach.* But the *Kulturkampf,* the struggle between the German empire of Bismarck and the Catholic Church, of which the Society was an early victim, brought the short-lived Jesuit incarnation of Maria Laach to an end.

In 1892, the Society sold the abbey to the Benedictine Congregation of Beuron, whose founders, the brothers Wolter, were in the process of emulating the wonderful success of Dom Prosper Guéranger's restoration of French monasticism across the Rhine.[2] Just over a decade later, the monks of Maria Laach gave Johannes Casel their habit and the religious name Odo, after St. Odo of Cluny, the initiator of the Cluniac monastery observance, the *ordo cluniacensis,* with its vision of monastic life as a continuation in the Church of the purification and renewal begun at Pentecost.

Odo Casel had entered Maria Laach on the eve of the finest period in its history. Under Ildefons Herwegen, who succeeded Dom Odo's first superior, Fidelis von Stotzingen, as abbot in 1913 and would remain in office until his death in 1948, Maria Laach became perhaps the single most important centre of the liturgical movement in the first half of the twentieth century. It promoted a grasp of the Liturgy of the Church at all levels, from the scholarly or scientific, as in the learned *Jahrbuch für Liturgiewissenschaft,* a journal started in 1921; through the less demanding *Ecclesia orans,* a series begun in 1918 of short books of the kind the French call *haute vulgarisation* – including Romano Guardini's best-selling

---

[2] See T. Bogler, *Maria Laach: Vergangenheit und Gegenwart der Abtei am Laacher See* (Munich 1961).

The Spirit of the Liturgy; right down to an annotated German-Latin Missal for parish use launched in 1929.

To say that Dom Odo was above all else a monk is to say that the story of his life – as distinct from his contribution to Catholic thought and sensibility in matters liturgical – is simply told. He was ordained priest on 17 September, 1911, and soon took the Liturgy and the Church Fathers as the ruling passions of his life – subject, however, to the yoke of Christ to which these interests were instrumentally subordinate. As he remarked to a correspondent: "It is not only study but the fact of fully sharing the life of Christ *in mysterio* [in the mystery] which is the final source of all knowledge."[3] In 1914 he completed a doctoral thesis for the Anselmianum, the Roman college of the Benedictines, on the eucharistic teaching of St. Justin Martyr, the second-century witness to the early Liturgy. Concerned to know more of the classical background to ancient theology, he followed up that thesis, in the approved German fashion, by a second doctorate, this time at Bonn, with the rather curious title *On the Mystical Silence of the Greek Philosophers* – an attempt, evidently, to evaluate the debts of the pagan Creek thinkers to the circumambient religion of the Hellenic and Hellenistic age.

The main bulk of Casel's considerable output of books and articles falls in the years 1921 to 1941.[4] His literary flow was assisted by the fact that in 1922 he had been exempted from conventual tasks by being named chaplain to the Benedictine nuns of Holy Cross abbey at Herstelle, between Paderborn and Kassel, on the river Weser. Odo Casel's best known work, *Das christliche Kultmysterium*, translated into many languages and into English in *The Mystery of Christian Worship and Other Writings* (ed. Burkhard Neunheuser, O.S.B., [London 1962]), neatly divides his period of intense productivity into two, by appearing conveniently close to its half-way mark, in 1932.

---

[3] Cited in A. Gozier, *Dom Casel* (Paris 1968), p. 18.

[4] For his writings, see P. Bienias, "Bibliographie von DDr. P. Odo Casel, O.S.B.," in A. Mayer, J. Quasten, B. Neunheuser (eds.), *Von christlichen Mysterium: Gesammelte Arbeiten zum Gedächtnis von Odo Casel, O.S.B.* (Düsseldorf 1951), pp. 363-75.

In 1948, at the comparatively early age of 61, weakened by the rigors of the years of war and post-war dearth and disruption, Odo Casel suffered a fatal stroke whilst acting as liturgical deacon at the Paschal vigil. He had just intoned the *Lumen Christi*, and the extraordinary congruence of his death with the teaching about the *Pascha Domini*, the Lord's Passover, sacramentally represented in the Liturgy, which he had given during his life, enabled the monks of Maria Laach to wax lyrical in their notification of his death to their fellow monastics:

> When he had first saluted aloud the light of Christ and was preparing to celebrate the Paschal praise, our beloved father in Christ, the liturgist of the sacred mystery and its mystagogue Odo Casel, monk of Maria Laach, his holocaust accomplished and himself passing over with his Lord during the holy night, entered into the blessed vision, being consummated in perfection by the mystery of Easter which he had given to the initiated.[5]

Not, however, that Dom Casel's life had simply passed in a mystical, patristical idyll of the sort the obituary notice describes. True, his own personality corresponded well enough, or so it would seem, to the impression left by their encomium. In his study of Casel, Gozier describes him as affectionate yet guarded in the expression of his own personality; a man of cell, choir stall, and research library; supremely controlled and thoughtful; someone who persuaded rather than tried to impose. And yet when Gozier adds, in the course of this character sketch, that Casel typically responded to attacks by deepening anew his own position, we naturally ask ourselves why so retiring a figure should be attacked at all.[6]

Here we begin to enter the realm of Dom Odo's *theology* – as distinct from his *service* – of the sacred Liturgy.[7] Living a

---

[5] A. Gozier, *Dom Casel* op. cit., p. 20.

[6] Ibid., 21-22.

[7] The best overall account, for readers of theological German, is A. Schilson, *Theologie als Sakramententheologie: Die Mysterientheologie Odo Casels* (Mainz 1982); the best short account in English is B. Neunheuser, "Masters in Israel: V., Odo Casel", *Clergy Review* (N. S.), LV. 3 (1970), pp. 194-212. A somewhat

cloistered life though he was, here was a man who could nonetheless preoccupy – and not in any unqualifiedly positive sense – a pope in writing an encyclical four months prior to Casel's death in March 1948, and of whose thought it could be said, in the context of the situation of Catholic theology in Germany a decade later, that it "seems to be the sole effective theological ferment of our time."[8]

Why did Odo Casel appear as a giant among theologians of the Liturgy and a figure raised up by Providence to salvage from perils the worship of the Church? The answer lies in the cultural conjuncture at which Odo Casel lived, a period that was shaped by forces from that eighteenth and nineteenth century world, or sequence of worlds, which, as we have seen, presented Koblenz and Maria Laach with so chequered a history. On the one hand was the neo-Classicism and rationalism of the eighteenth century; on the other, the Romanticism, nationalism and Expressionism of the nineteenth. Translated into terms of influence on the Liturgy, these meant, in the first case, formalism and a view of the Church's worship as primarily didactic and ethical – a vehicle for instruction and moral uplift, and, in the second, a sentimentalized picture of the Liturgy which would see it as a celebration and release of feeling (Romanticism), an embodiment of ethnic and cultural community (nationalism), and a manifestation of gifts already bestowed, along with wounds needing healing, in the individual self (Expressionism). Offered this choice between Scylla and Charybdis – a rationalized Liturgy or a sentimentalized one – Odo Casel divined that a true approach to the Liturgy must avoid both by heading out for deeper waters. What was needed, and what Casel set out to provide, was an evangelical ontology of the Liturgy, an account of the Liturgy as an epiphany of the Gospel of grace which would throw light on the unique reality which the

---

impressionistic account by an Anglican writer can be found in G. Guiver, C.R., *Pursuing the Mystery: Worship and Daily Life as Presences of God* (London 1996), pp. 55-97, especially.

[8] J. Pinsk, *Catholicisme allemand* (Paris 1956), cited in J. Gaillard, "La théologie des Mystères," *Revue Thomiste* 57.3 (1957), p. 510.

Liturgy both is and also brings into our midst. His *Mysterienlehre* – the "doctrine of the Mysteries," his mysteric theology of the Liturgy – is precisely that: an *ontology* of the Liturgy.

Aptly, then, writing in 1968, when the Church in France reached, surely, its lowest point of self-confidence since the Revolution – not least because of the collapse of its traditional worship – André Gozier could conclude that, although Casel's analytic and systematic powers were perhaps insufficient for the full attaining of the goal he had set himself, nevertheless,

> his feeling for the history of religion; his affinity with antiquity; his truly exceptional knowledge of the Church Fathers; his unequaled liturgical sense; his monastic spirit, supported as this was by an extremely pure life of worship – in brief, so many factors joined together in just one human being, prepared him in extraordinary fashion to attempt that theology of the Liturgy of which our own time stands in so great need. [9]

What, then, is Odo Casel's teaching on the nature of the liturgy? Its key word is *mysterion, Mysterium,* "the Mystery."[10] To grasp the sense of that word as applied to the Church's worship, we have to appreciate the more primordial sense in which it must be used – with Scripture and the Fathers – of God, Christ, and the activity of Christ. The primordial Mystery is God himself, who in his self-revelation remains mysterious because, divine as he is in his being, he must be inaccessible to our intelligence until, that is, he makes himself known to us by his grace. Next, the definitive expression or epiphany of this Mystery is Christ, who makes the saving plan of God manifest not only because he is in his own person the presence of God but also because he is the fulfillment of that plan. And furthermore, Christ's epiphanic character as the expression of the Mystery of God is itself realized in his acts, each of which, from the Incarnation to the Ascension, can also be called a "mystery" inasmuch as in his deeds and gestures the divine Glory

---

[9] Gozier, *Dom Casel,* op. cit., p. 25.
[10] O. Casel, "Theologische Philologie zum Worte 'Mysterium,'" *Jahrbuch für Liturgiewissenschaft* 15 (1941), pp. 269-305.

makes itself known, though in an inexhaustible way, through his humanity. It is the interrelation of these three senses of "mystery" – the Mystery as God, as Christ, and as the actions of Christ – which for Casel explains why it is that the Church never claims to lead humanity to salvation by word alone, but only by words thoroughly integrated with sacred actions.[11]

This brings us to the topic of the mystery of the Liturgy. The cultic mystery, the mystery of worship, *das Kultmysterium*, is the presence of the saving "theandric"–divine-human – actions of Christ under the veil of symbols; it is the God-man, the Saviour, pursuing his activity through time and space in such a way that, thanks to the rite, what was once achieved in Palestine can now reach all humanity.[12] Casel goes beyond any merely functional or phenomenological account of the Liturgy, such as sociologists and cultural anthropologists might supply, or pastoral strategists and planners of liturgical ceremonies in the Church. He goes beyond to that ontology of the Gospel in whose terms alone the proper function of Christian worship and its true visage can be seen. The Liturgy *is* – the question, to repeat, must be posed as one of ontology, of foundational being – the mystery of Christ in the worship of the Church. The word "liturgy" draws attention to the Church's active role in the construction of worship – which, clearly enough, it would be foolish (indeed impossible!) to deny. The word "mystery" qualifies, however, all "constructivist" accounts of what Liturgy is by insisting that the essence of the sacred action is the redemptive work which Christ continues in his Church by means of the rite.

The Liturgy in its total unfolding in the Church year renders present, according to Casel, not simply the effects of Christ's redemptive activity – the grace conferred by it, its fruit, or result, or efficacy – but the Saviour's redemptive action *in itself*. His redeeming work, from Annunciation to Glorification, is not

---

[11] O. Casel, "Mysteriengegenwart," *Jahrbuch für Liturgiewissenschaft* 8 (1928), pp. 145-224.
[12] Idem., *Die Liturgie als Mysterienfeier*, = *Ecclesia Orans* 9 (Freiburg im Breisgau 1922); idem., *Glaube, Gnosis, Mysterium* (Münster 1941).

present under the formality of the historical events in which it was, once for all, embodied. Rather, it is present sacramentally – but, since "sacramentally" here does not mean "less really," this is simply an alteration in the mode of being of those actions the Word incarnate carried out for our salvation and which make him who he is as our Saviour. Indeed, one could even regard the actions of the God-man as *more* really present in the liturgical mystery than in their original historical embodiment, since they were not then fully invested with the power of the Holy Spirit sent by the Father to crown the work of the Son in Pentecostal wind and flames. Evidently, such a view enhances considerably the honour in which the cycle of the Liturgy should be held, but it also affects – more subtly yet unmistakably – our approach to the most central and sacred act of worship the Church performs, the Mass-rite itself. For Casel, what is present in the eucharistic sacrifice is not so much Christ in the saving effects that follow from his redeeming work (as the Latin church prays so often in a collect, "may we so venerate the sacred mysteries of thy Body and Blood that we may constantly feel in our lives the *effects* [*fructum*, fruit] of thy redemption") as it is that redeeming work *itself* – *the* action of the Passover of Christ, the death passing into resurrection triumph, from which those gracious effects, that salutary fruit, proceed.[13]

This understanding should alert us to the fact that, as his contemporaries were well aware, Casel was not saying quite the same thing as other theologians of his, or an earlier day, nor was his position in every respect borne out by the texts of the Latin liturgical books themselves. This did not unduly worry him, because, so far as other theologians were concerned, he believed that he had the *gravior pars* of the Fathers on his side. With regard to the liturgical sources, he considered that his account could make sense of texts that, *prima facie*, did not offer succour to supporters of the *Mysterienlehre*, whereas his opponents would have the greatest difficulty in making head or tail of other and perhaps

---

[13] Idem., "Art und Sinn der ältesten christlichen Osterfeier," *Jahrbuch für Liturgiewissenschaft* 14 (1938), pp. 1-78.

weightier texts eloquent in speaking for his cause. To investigate a little of how even theologians basically sympathetic to his fundamental approach could differ from him will lead us into the more important question of whether, as some people believed, Odo Casel and the school of Maria Laach had been impugned, or even implicitly condemned, by the encyclical of Pope Pius XII on the liturgical movement, *Mediator Dei*.

The doctrine of the mysteries proposed by Dom Odo did not meet with universal acclaim. Theologians close to his mind-set, like the German-born abbot of Buckfast, Dom Anscar Vonier, and the French secular priest – a disciple of Vonier's in questions of eucharistic theology – Eugene Masure, did not rally fully to Casel's insistence that the entire Paschal mystery, rather than simply the Crucified and the fruits of his bloody Passion, is made present in the Mass – and therewith, as the Eucharist is celebrated week in, week out, day in, day out, in the liturgical year, the other mysteries of the Lord's incarnation, life, glorification likewise.[14] Casel replied that Trent itself called the Mass the *repraesentatio* of the "victory and triumph of the death," and that unless the Holy Eucharist rendered present the entire economy of salvation in Christ it could hardly be called *sacramentum salutis*, the "sacrament of our salvation."

Further removed from Casel were other theologians, of whom the best known is the Bavarian Karl Adam, who survived long enough to be invited as a *peritus* to the opening session of Vatican II.[15] These scholars argued that what is represented in the cult and renders it sanctifying in our regard is not the redeeming action of the Lord but only his "oblatory" and "propitiatory" will, his willingness to sacrifice himself for us. The sacramental Liturgy, on this view, actualizes in our present the psychological attitude

---

[14] A. Vonier, *A Key to the Doctrine of the Holy Eucharist* (London 1925); E. Masure, *Le Sacrifice du Chef* (Paris 1944).
[15] K. Adam, "Les bases dogmatiques de la Liturgie," *Questions liturgiques et paroissiales* XXII (1937), pp. 3-18; 75-92; 147-158. And see more widely, J. Butler, "Die Mysterienthese der Laacher Schule im Zusammenhang scholasticher Theologie", *Zeitschrift für katholische Theologie* LIX (1935), pp. 546-71.

subjacent to Christ's redemptive deeds. Casel pointed out however, that what the Church teaches is that we are saved by Christ's redeeming *work* in all its objectivity, and not simply by his redeeming *will*. Still, as a monk of the Belgian monastery of Steenbrugge, Dom Eloi Dekkers, explained in the issue of *La Maison-Dieu* dedicated to Casel in the aftermath of his sudden death, it is not the *quod*, the "what", of Casel's talk of the presence of the mystery that other theologians cavilled at, so much as the *quomodo*, the "how."[16] Many Catholic divines had no desire to find themselves facing a new onslaught of Protestant criticism, or a barrage of expressions of Protestant anxieties, caused by the way Casel might be construed as teaching a reiteration, a repeating, of the saving acts of the Lord in the Church's rites. "Today Christ is born for us": surely some less controversial account could be found of the *hodie* texts of the Roman Liturgy than this. Was it sufficient to ascribe to the liturgical actions a "real efficacy," or might it be necessary, after all, to go all the way with Casel, and speak instead of an "efficacious reality" present in the cult?

Those were the nuanced terms in which Casel was confronted by possibly the most able of his interlocutors, the Braunsberg theologian Gottlieb Söhngen, the very titles of whose works – *Symbol and Reality in the Cultic Mystery* and *The Essential Structure of the Mystery* – in any case betray the influence of Casel's thought.[17] This perspective did not, however reconcile the theologians of Maria Laach to Söhngen's claim that the sacrament is something happening *in our regard*, rather than something *in itself.* The sacramental sign, they argued, is the ritual face of the redemptive act of Christ in its plenary reality, and not simply a communication of grace. Söhngen's theology might be more dynamic in its emphasis on the sacramental Liturgy's effect on us, but the price paid was too high: a turn to psychology and even anthropocentrism which the objectivity of an authentic liturgical

---

[16] E. Dekkers, "La liturgie, Mystère chrétien," *La Maison Dieu* 14 (1948), pp. 30-64.

[17] G. Söhngen, *Symbol und Wirklichkeit im Kultmysterium* (Bonn 1937); idem., *Der Wesensaufbau des Mysteriums* (Bonn 1938). His thinking was subsequently summarised in *Das sakramentale Wesen des Messopfers* (Essen 1946).

existence would ultimately be unable to withstand.[18] As I shall suggest in my conclusion, these were prophetic words. In addition to the *quod* and the *quomodo*, the "what" and the "how" of Casel's *Mysterienlehre*, questions were also asked about the *ubi*, the "where" of its application. His interlocutors – and foremost here was the Münster dogmatician Michael Schmaus – suggested that while Dom Odo's theology fitted well enough into the context of the Mass, it was somewhat ill at ease, not to say out of place, with Baptism. Why, for instance, on the mystery-presence theory, were not *all* the sacraments sacrifices?[19] Casel's immediate reply was that in Baptism (the other sacrament chiefly at issue), the death of Christ was indeed present – but not in formally sacrificial terms. The trouble was, however, that if all the gains of clarity provided by Christian scholasticism were not to be lost to the Latin church, Maria Laach's insistence that not only all the sacraments but also the sacramentals and the Liturgy of the Hours manifested the mysteric presence of the saving acts of Christ seemed too sweeping an assertion.

Casel, nevertheless, was reluctant to abandon for this reason what he saw as a real recovery of that more global view which the Fathers had entertained of the relation between the divine being in its incarnate action on the one hand and *all* the rites of the Church on the other. We are speaking here of a period when Thomism – admittedly, in very different guises – was the dominant mode of articulating theological doctrine in the Catholic Church. The difficulty of persuading neo-scholastic divines that Maria Laach could be accommodated within the Thomist synthesis had already been raised in 1928 by the German Jesuit Johann Baptist Umberg, Casel's earliest and fiercest opponent.[20] This only added to the ecclesiastical-political insecurities of Casel's position. It is fair to add, however, that others, like the great Breslau sacramentologist Bernhard Poschmann looked more favorably on Casel's

---

[18] I am paraphrasing here Dekkers, "La liturgie, Mystère chrétien," art. cit., p. 56.

[19] M. Schmaus, "Liturgische Erneurung," *Catholica* VI (1937).

[20] J.B. Umberg, S.J., "'Mysterien' Frommigkeit?" *Zeitschrift für Aszese und Mystik* 1 (1926), pp. 351-66.

protestation that St. Thomas was too soaked in the spirit of the Fathers to take any other view than his own – though even Poschmann balked at the idea that Thomas had affirmed in explicit language the presence of the redeeming act itself in the sacraments, even in the Eucharist.[21]

These anxieties came to a head with the publication of *Mediator Dei*, which left the brewing soup, it must be said, hotter but hardly clearer. At the Rhineland abbey, the latest encyclical from Rome was received with jubilation as the vindication of Casel, now some months gone to the Lord, and of the Maria Laach school as a whole. For *Mediator Dei* taught that the Liturgy was not simply a canonically ordered set of rubrics for Church ceremonies, but the public worship Christ gives to the Father, his mystical Body conjoined with him in that act. Pope Pius XII spoke of the presence of Christ in the whole liturgical action, especially in regard to the Church year. On the eucharistic sacrifice, though his terminology was that of the post-Tridentine schools, his entire account, it was said, breathed that same spirit of "mystical realism" as blew at Maria Laach. In the Mass, so *Mediator Dei* declared, "id agit quod jam in Cruce fecit," "he does what once on the Cross he did" – and what is this if not an affirmation that the same redemptive gesture is at stake, but in different modes?

Imagine, then, the horror of abbot and monks when other Catholic commentators drew the quite contrary conclusion that "the Rhenish innovators" had suffered a body blow from which they would never recover. It was true that *Mediator Dei* had fulminated against those who so exalted the objective holiness of the Liturgy as to leave no place for subjective – personal, devotional – piety, individual prayer and asceticism in the Christian life. The posthumous defenders of Casel replied that, whatever some exaggerated voices might mistakenly have suggested, Maria Laach espoused no "hyperliturgism." Quite apart from those passages in Casel's writing in which he had spoken of the need for the harmonious integration of objective and

---

[21] B. Poschmann, "Mysteriengegenwart im Licht des hl. Thomas," *Theologische Quartalschrift* 116 (1935), pp. 53-116.

subjective piety, and the requirement on all worshipers to participate in as personal a way as possible in the mysteries, and the sense in which the Liturgy could launch and sustain a life of devotion in other respects, one only had to consider the austere, sacrificial, ascetic ethos of the Maria Laach community itself, and Casel's own exemplarily recollected, detached, disciplined life. But then there was also the notorious paragraph 176 in *Mediator Dei* which spoke of how in the liturgical cycle the mysteries of Christ are "still now constantly present and active, not in the vague and nebulous way which certain recent writers describe [here a particularly uncomplimentary verb, *effutire*, was used, best translated perhaps as "blether"], but as Catholic doctrine teaches us."

Again, the guardians of Casel's memory responded that the cap did not fit. A Christian esotericism or occultism had never been his intention. No more did he propose to play down the historical Christ of Judaea and Galilee over against the glorious Christ of the Liturgy (another of the encyclical's *bêtes noirs*), for, in Caselian thought, what the mystery of worship reveals to us is the entire meaning of the historic deeds, precisely, of the now glorified Saviour. Maria Laach responded to the adverse interpretation of *Mediator Dei*, then, with stout denial. The notions the pope had criticized so severely were not to be found in the writings of the school; the most they would grant was, "Man kann sie hineinlesen" – it was possible to read them back into them.[22]

In fact, so confident were Casel's admirers that his opponents had misread the nature of the papal intervention that they sought, through the good offices of the archbishop of Salzburg, a clarification of the position from the Roman dicasteries. In this they were disappointed, for the letter of the Holy Office, published in diverse organs in 1948 and 1949, very definitely fence-sat. However, the influential Italian bishop-theologian of Pius XII's later years, Antonio Bernareggi of Bergamo, agreed with the abbot of Maria Laach that the letter

---

[22] Dom Jean Hild, "L'encyclique *Mediator Dei* et le mouvement liturgique de Maria Laach," *Maison Dieu* 14 (1948), pp. 15-29.

presented the encyclical as not seeking to exclude all attempt to explain the Liturgy as a representation of the life of Christ, but rather inviting a further elucidation of the relation between the "historic mystery" and the "liturgical mysteries."[23]

The effect of the cloud – or was it rather just a silver lining? – which descended over Casel's work at this time was that, while his writings never ceased to be used and studied by historians of the Liturgy and of modern Catholic theology, it was possible to detect a certain reluctance to quote them directly. Slowly, however, Caselian ideas, I would suggest, took deeper hold in the magisterial tradition: one can find them especially in the opening chapter of the Constitution on the Sacred Liturgy of the Second Vatican Council, as well as in what that document has to say about the sacrifice of the Mass, the divine Office, and the liturgical year, and they resurface in Pope Paul VI's letter on the eucharist, *Mysterium Fidei*. Nonetheless, the reluctance to treat Dom Odo Casel as one of the great fathers, indeed I would say *the* great father, of the twentieth century liturgical movement made it easy for those who had quite different agendas for the future of that movement, and appealed to other, less crucial, sections of the Conciliar constitution – those, namely dealing with the theme of the pastoral adaptation of the rites – to push the entire liturgical life of Western Catholicism in a direction which, I do not think it excessive to say, Casel would abhor.

In the mainstream of English-language sacramental theology today, it is not, I think, rash to claim that the unique ontology of the sacraments has largely been lost to view. By and large, the sacraments are treated as symbols which have a power to focus the

---

[23] A. Bernareggi, "Il movimento liturgico da Pio X alla *Mediator Dei*," *Scuola Cattolica* 78 [1950]; cited in B. Neunheuser, O.S.B., "Mysteriengegenwart: ein Theologoumenon inmitten des Gesprächs ," *Archiv für Liturgiewissenschaft* III. 1 (1953), pp. 104-122, and here at pp. 109-110. See further idem., "Der positiv Sinn der päpstlichen Grenzsetzung in der Enzyklika *Mediator Dei*", in A. Mayer, J. Quasten, B. Neunheuser, *Vom christlichen Mysterium*, op. cit., pp. 344-362. The abbatial contribution was B. Ebel, O.S.B., "Das Mysterium im Lichte der Enzyklika *Mediator Dei*," *Anima* 3 (1948), 294-307.

lessons of Christian experience – or simply of human experience as such – in a fashion that lends itself to the furtherance of God's plan for humankind. We can note, in the first place, a marked tendency to remove the distinction between the sacramental and the non-sacramental domains. The world, so Karl Rahner proclaimed, is the sacrament of God, and if that phrase could indeed be given an orthodox meaning, more usually it had the effect of undermining a sense of the distinctiveness of sacramental reality. By eliding the distinction between natural and supernatural, and hence between secular and sacred, world and Church, God was said to be immediately present by his grace to all situations of human life. If this was over-optimistic – since the Incarnation and the redemption of humanity by Christ do not of themselves entail, evidently, that all human life is exempt from evil and its consequence in alienation from God – the idea might be reformulated along the lines of the claim (and here I quote Michael Taylor) that "grace happens wherever human life is lived and celebrated *authentically*" – which has, however, the equally undesirable effect of reducing Christian sacramentalism to a humanism.[24] Where the concept of the sacred is retained, as in Joseph Martos' work, the content given that notion could be filled, as it is there, with materials provided by phenomenologists of religion – any religion – rather than by Christian philosophers and theologians, in which case it could be concluded that if the seven Christian sacraments as we have them do not lead effectively to the sacred nowadays, and other symbolic actions do, the Church's sacramental system can and should be thoroughgoingly redesigned.[25]

The acceptance within sacramental theology of an understanding of grace in which grace is found more fundamentally in human experience generally or, at best, in

---

[24] M.J. Taylor, S.J., "Introduction", in idem. (ed.), *The Sacraments: Readings in Contemporary Sacramental Theology*, (New York 1981), p. ix. Emphasis added. It is only fair to note that Taylor qualifies his remarks by explaining that he is speaking of humanity after the Incarnation and Atonement.

[25] J. Martos, *Doors to the Sacred: A Historical Introduction to the Sacraments in the Catholic Church* (New York 1981).

Christian experience at large than it is in sacramental experience in particular is, in postconciliar theology, often married with an emphasis on liturgical action as a rehearsal or retelling of the narrative or story which Christians use to interpret experience and reach the conclusion that experience is indeed already gracious. Thus Tad Guzie has written: "A sacrament is a festive action in which Christians assemble to celebrate their lived experience and to call to heart their common story."[26] The writer, later in the same passage, goes on to illustrate a further theme in what I would call the "flight from sacramental ontology," and that is the adoption, in place of the notion of divinely effective sacred signs, of the idea, rather, of anthropologically effective symbols. As Guzie explains: "The action is a symbol of God's care for us in Christ. Enacting the symbol brings us closer to one another in the Church and to the Lord who is there for us." Such a statement is, once again, capable of an orthodox interpretation, yet such an interpretation is far from imposing itself. Some writers indeed more or less exclude any reading of sacramental causality which goes beyond the sphere of human consciousness or social action, refusing to invoke a direct divine action in the sacramental sign.

In the perspective of liberation theology, for instance, Juan Luis Segundo has this to say: a sacrament is "the community's way of reactivating and deepening our interpretation of, and commitment to, the historical process geared toward man's liberation."[27] Here the key liberationist idea that God is not so much, as in Karl Rahner's transcendental theology, the presence which the world mediates as he is the future of the historical process, gives a particular twist to the idea of sacraments as symbolic signs. Rather than being, as for Guzie, signs of the blessings of God already given in experience before we come to the liturgy, sacraments here become signs of the future blessings – certainly not found in the Liturgy here and now or in ritual at any time – to which engagement by faith in liberationist praxis directs

---

[26] T. Guzie, *The Book of Sacramental Basics* (New York – Ramsey 1981), p.53.

[27] J.L. Segundo, *The Sacraments Today* (Et Maryknoll 1975 = *A Theology for Artisans of a New Humanity*, vol. IV), p. 59.

us. Alternatively, for sacramental theologians less interested in radical politics, and, perhaps, like many people in modern Western society, tempted to abandon the public realm altogether in favor of an exclusive stress on the private values of personal relationship, the experience to which the symbolic signs point may be, as for Bernard Cooke, that of intimacy, friendship and small-scale interrelations – which is why in his work the author can put forward the unprecedented thesis that marriage, rather than the Holy Eucharist or Baptism, is the fundamental sacrament in the Church.[28]

Even with writers whose profound and detailed knowledge of the actual history of sacramental worship saves them from such *bêtises* (I have in mind David Power of The Catholic University of America), we find a definite tendency to avoid the language of intrinsic sacramental efficacy – even the real efficacy of Söhngen, never mind the efficacious reality spoken of by Casel – and, with this, to suppress any suggestion that there is a distinct sacramental ontology which raises the common being we experience in the created order – albeit a created order situated within a gracious plan – to a new intensity, a new level. For Power, "The liturgy is an action wherein the testimony of God is heard and appropriated, the experience of the community is transformed, and a godly presence disclosed."[29] At least this statement, unlike that of Segundo, allows us to think that the sacraments are meant to lead their recipients to encounter the mystery of the Father, through Christ, in the Holy Spirit. Yet Power's definition of what the Liturgy is can only strike us, in comparison with the work, above all, of Casel, but also, for that matter, of all the Catholic theologians who were his inter-war contemporaries, as remarkably weak on the question of the divine prevenience, the priority in the sacred Liturgy of God's initiative – which is what makes the Liturgy "sacred," makes it a moment or series of moments in

---

[28] B. Cooke, *Sacraments and Sacramentality* (Mystic, Conn. 1983).

[29] D.N. Power, *Unsearchable Riches: The Symbolic Nature of the Liturgy* (New York 1984), p. 146.

which we ourselves are sought out by the God of salvation and find the divine life, righteousness and peace bestowed upon us.

What has gone wrong in English-speaking sacramental theology is, it would seem, a flight, more or less precipitate, more or less pronounced, from that notion of the unique and uniquely sacred ontology of the sacramental Liturgy which Odo Casel took it as his life work to both identify and strengthen in the Latin church of his day. The reasons for, or causes of, this flight are various: among them the near-collapse of Christian metaphysics and the characteristic recourse of our culture to psychology and sociology for the understanding of reality. But a deficient liturgical practice, mostly abusive of the intentions of the liturgical reformers of the 1960s and 1970s – but sometimes taking its cue from weaknesses in their work – must also figure prominently on any such list.

The Conciliar Constitution on the Sacred Liturgy shows the mark of diverse hands. It contains passages where one can see, as through a palimpsest, the writings of Casel, the influence of Maria Laach. It also contains other very different clauses where the zeal for ongoing adaptation of the Roman rite by the more radical figures on the postconciliar *Consilium* or by pastoral liturgists on the commissions of the national bishops' conferences could look for inspiration and succour. But the word "pastoral" is a slippery one, for it cannot be good shepherding to short-sell the Christian people by providing them with forms of worship that may be immediately intelligible and furnish group bonding, but also fail to nourish at depth precisely because the deep being of the Liturgy, that sacred ontology in whose exploration Casel spent his energies, is not respected.

In the past, pastoral liturgists have been – at least at times – more acute. The commemorative issue of *La Maison-Dieu* on Odo Casel is preceded by an editorial note which in retrospect one finds not only moving but also uncannily prophetic. The journal of the Centre de Pastorale Liturgique at Paris was mainly run by the diocesan clergy of France, assisted by Dominican friars. In their note they say of Casel and the school of Maria Laach that, without their contribution, the pastoral efforts of liturgical specialists "aurait vite perdu sa fraîcheur et comme sa densité spécifique" – would have "quickly lost its freshness and, as it were, its specific density;" "pour être ravalé au niveau d'une très quelconque pastorale" – to be "lowered to the level of a very mediocre pastoral policy indeed;" "d'un mouvement, au sense le plus péjoratif du terme qui évoque celui d'une agitation" – to that of "a movement in the most pejorative sense of that word, which is not far from signifying just an agitation."[30] The applicability of those words to our situation today hardly needs underlining – except to say that, if the *équipe* of the Centre were right, the liturgical theology of Dom Odo Casel must be a much-needed tract for our times.

---

[30] *Maison-Dieu* 14 (1948), p. 4.

IX

A Tale of Two Documents: *Sacrosanctum Concilium* and *Mediator Dei*

The semi-centenary of *Mediator Dei*, once hailed as the "Charter" of the Liturgical Movement came and went in 1997 with no great brouhaha. Yet in seeking a title for an essay comparing that Letter with the now much more celebrated document on Christian worship from Vatican II, I put the name of the Conciliar Liturgy Constitution of 1963 before that of the 1947 papal encyclical almost entirely for reasons of euphony. For not only chronologically but also in terms of theological substance – at any rate in most if not all respects (as I hope to show) – the primacy belongs to *Mediator Dei*. In saying as much, I am no doubt condemning myself in some Catholic quarters (does not *Mediator Dei* represent the closed world of the last of the Pian popes, from which we were graciously emancipated by Vatican II?), just as I am simultaneously endearing myself in others (was not *Sacrosanctum Concilium*, through the liturgical revolution it unleashed, the cause, in the area of worship, of our present woes?). The way we look back at these two major documents of twentieth century Catholicism can hardly be unaffected by how we evaluate the post-Conciliar epoch in the Catholic Church both in general and in the specifically liturgical domain. And here the opening words of Charles Dickens' *A Tale of Two Cities* are surely apposite. Summing up the wildly conflicting judgments by contemporaries on the revolutionary events initiated by the summoning of the Estates-General in France, Dickens wrote:

> It was the best of times, it was the worst of times, it was the age of wisdom, it was the age of foolishness, it was the epoch of belief, it was the epoch of incredulity, it was the season of Light, it was the season of Darkness...[1]

---

[1] Charles Dickens, *A Tale of Two Cities*, I. 1.

Dickens himself, as the ironic tone of this passage suggests, believed the revolutionary period to be neither. What he *did* believe it to be I shall return to – for the analogy between the Great Revolution of the West and the ecclesial revolution of the last generation is not without value – at the close of my analysis. For the moment, however, we can register the fact, echoing Dickens' overture, that, for the Church historian, the likelihood that *any* time in the Church's life consists of nothing but light celestial is as great as the likelihood that any time in the Church's life is made up of unremitting gloom. Which is to say: that likelihood is very small indeed. My contention that *Mediator Dei* is, in most aspects, a more substantial document than is *Sacrosanctum Concilium* is founded not on a priori preference for things pre-Conciliar, but rather on exploration of the well-foundedness and adequacy of the ideas it uses.

Before embarking on an exposition of those ideas, and indeed of the smaller set represented by the Conciliar Constitution as well, one caveat, already hinted at, should be stressed, and two others should be entered.

In one major respect I find the theology of the Liturgy in *Sacrosanctum Concilium* to enjoy a distinct advantage over the understanding of worship in *Mediator Dei* and that is in its more pronounced orientation towards the eschaton, the Lord's Parousia at the end of time. A theme almost entirely absent from Pius XII's encyclical, and hardly central, despite the Conciliar Constitution, to the liturgical consciousness of Western Catholics using the reformed rites, it is highly conspicuous, not to say the predominant consideration, in what is perhaps the most impressive, if little noticed, theology of the Liturgy produced in the present pontificate by an author later commissioned, and not, I think, accidentally, to write the concluding book of the 1992 *Catechism*, the section on prayer.[2]

If that is a subject to which I must return, it will by contrast suffice here just to note my two remaining caveats to the overall

---

[2] Jean Corbon, *The Wellspring of Worship* (Et Mahwah, N. J., 1988).

judgment that *Mediator Dei* provides more solid nourishment for the liturgical life than does the Liturgy constitution of the Council itself.

In terms of modern Catholicism's history, it is perfectly defensible to say that, when we compare *Sacrosanctum Concilium* with *Mediator Dei* we are not, strictly speaking, comparing like with like. The two documents do not belong to the same *genre*. In so saying that I do not have in mind the fact that one is conciliar and the other papal in its formal authority. My point is to do with the kind of text that the authors envisaged. Pius XII intended to offer an evaluation of the Liturgical Movement of his time by painting a doctrinal portrait of what the sacred Liturgy is. He proposed to set forth what was salutary, as distinct from what was either exaggerated or defective, about that movement by providing a fully rounded picture of the Liturgy in terms of theological doctrine. He aimed to correct certain distortions in people's minds, as well as abuses in the manner of liturgical celebration, by giving a theologically true account of the nature of Christian worship. His intervention, we can say, was essentially theoretical, though it had, to be sure, a practical finality. The Fathers of the Second Vatican Council, by contrast, intended to provide guidelines for an imminent reform of the liturgical books and a re-formulation of liturgical law. To this end they evidently thought it sufficient to preface their practical proposals with a relatively brief theological prologue, though they also reverted on occasion to wider doctrinal considerations when introducing particular topics of reform: the rite of Mass, the Church calendar, the divine Office. Accordingly, we can say that the intervention of the bishops was essentially practical, though they bore in mind certain theoretical principles. Evidently, one cannot criticise *Sacrosanctum Concilium* for not fulfilling a promise the Fathers of Vatican II never gave; although with the benefit of hindsight one could regret that the predominantly practical character of their proposals, made as these were in a culturally pragmatist age, was not balanced in advance by a fuller theology of worship, drawing not least on *Mediator Dei*.

There is one more caveat I would register against my thesis that, even when we have recognised the disparity in genre of the two documents, *Mediator Dei* is in most respects theologically superior to the Conciliar Constitution. The remaining caveat is that this contrast should not be exploited polemically, creating conflict, *polemos*, from which our word "polemical" derives, by setting one at the throat of the other. The difference between *Mediator Dei* and *Sacrosanctum Concilium* is, to revert to the Dickens comparison, not the difference between Louis XIV and Robespierre. At most it is the difference between Cardinal Richelieu and the Constituent Assembly. Or, to put the point less allusively, in terms of the spectrum of opinion about the Liturgy in their periods, the 1940s and the 1960s respectively, *Mediator Dei* is, against a background of liturgical conservatism, much of it by inertia, a moderately reformist document – though, as we shall see, it contains the ingredients of a recipe for a neo-orthodox reaction to liturgical reform. *Sacrosanctum Concilium* is, against a background of growing liturgical radicalism, a largely traditional document – though at the same time it carried within it, encased in the innocuous language of pastoral welfare, the seeds of its own destruction.

In this essay, I shall concentrate on *three main differences* in the conception of the Liturgy stated or implicit in *Sacrosanctum Concilium* and *Mediator Dei*. And these are: first, the rôle of a theology of devotion, or what the encyclical calls the primacy of "internal worship", in Pius XII's letter; secondly, the principle stated there that all liturgical ages of the New Testament Church, and not simply that of the primitive development of the rites, are open to God; and thirdly, and this is the point on which I hold *Mediator Dei* to be *inferior* to *Sacrosanctum Concilium*, the exclusively realised eschatology, invoked by the papal letter to describe the ultimate reality we have to do with in the liturgical action. This is the way, already mentioned, *Mediator Dei* views that more-than-human reality made available in the sacred Liturgy, and *rendering* it sacred, indeed – as the *present* most holy being of Jesus Christ, the God-man, in the fulness of his saving activity for us, to the effective exclusion of any concern for the Liturgy as the realised anticipation of the future Parousia of the Lord: his coming with all his saints to inaugurate the final plenitude which that all-sufficient saving activity makes possible, the reign of the Father in the Holy Spirit, not the new heavens only, which we have already through the access of those redeemed by Christ to the Beatific Vision, but also the new earth.

Exposition of those three main points must, however, be topped and tailed. I shall *round them off* by drawing attention to two other less structural but by no means unimportant differences of emphasis between the two documents. But beforehand, I want to *preface* them by mentioning one enormous fact which the two texts have in common and which alone, despite the discontinuities they may contain, sets them aside from many alternative statements of the rationale of worship available in today's Church, and that fact is the *soteriological perspective* in which they see all liturgical action, the way they treat the Liturgy as essentially in function of *Christian salvation.*

So to that I now turn. *Sacrosanctum Concilium,* after an initial paragraph outlining why a Council with the aims Vatican II set itself should be concerned with the Liturgy at all, and *Mediator Dei* from the very outset, furnish a rationale for liturgical celebration which is entirely salvational in character. So far from providing an explanation of why there is a Liturgy couched in the terms of sociology, or religious philosophy, or political ethics – all of which could well have predominated in subsequent discussion – both documents begin by asserting that the Liturgy only makes sense in relation to salvation. In the papal letter, it is by the Liturgy especially that "the Church at the bidding of her Founder continues the priestly office of Jesus Christ" –[3] a priestly office undertaken, so the pope explained, in order to

> re-establish between men and their Creator the order that sin
> had upset and so bring back to their heavenly Father, first

---

[3] *Mediator Dei,* 3.

beginning and last end of all creatures, the unhappy progeny of Adam.[4]

The Sacrifice of the altar, the sacraments, and the Liturgy of the hours considered (and here the twelfth Pius quoted the eleventh) as expressive of the thanksgiving, praise, petition and expiation prayed by Christ's own mystical body, prolong the self-offering of the incarnate Word by which, when on earth, he set the sinful on the way of return to the Father, and these sacred actions do so, moreover, while at the same time enabling believers to – in the words of that crucial opening paragraph of the letter – co-operate

> personally in their sanctification, making their own the holiness that springs from the blood of the unspotted Lamb.[5]

That notion of personal co-operation, what the Greek Fathers call *synergia*, co-working, whereby I must make a spiritual effort in the Liturgy congruent with God's outreach to me there in the sacred signs, will be highly relevant to what I have called Pius XII's theology of devotion, as we shall see.

Just the same salvational perspective, seeing the Liturgy as the continuing expression of the Father's offer to us of new holiness through the sacrificial death of Christ, is also the burden of the early sections of *Sacrosanctum Concilium* as well. And in fact, the doctrinal link between the Liturgy and salvation is, if anything, tightened in those early paragraphs of the Liturgy Constitution, by citation of a "Secret" prayer for the time after Pentecost which has it that, through the Liturgy, *opus nostrae Redemptionis exercetur*, "the work of our redemption is carried on".[6]

In both documents, then, we are worlds away from any sub-theological ideology of the Liturgy for which the purpose of the Liturgy might be, for instance, to affirm the group identity of the assembly; to express gender, class or ethnic belonging; or to recognise in symbolic play the presence or action of the divine in secular life and reality. There are, no doubt, legitimate senses in

---

[4] Ibid., 1.

[5] Ibid.

[6] *Sacrosanctum Concilium* 2, cf. 6.

which the Liturgy might be said, incidentally and *per accidens*, to perform some or, on occasion, even all of these job-descriptions, but none of them get anywhere hear stating what the essential rationale of the Liturgy is.

Mediator Dei and *Sacrosanctum Concilium* come identifiably, then, from the same stable; or to put the point in more theological language, both are recognisable expressions of the doctrine of worship which has always been implicit in the sense of faith of the Church.

Let us consider now the chief points of difference in this tale of two documents, and first of all, as between the two respects in which *Mediator Dei* scores when compared with its successor text, what I have termed the "theology of devotion" which plays so crucial a part in the way Pius XII saw liturgical participation as offering us the opportunity for *synergia*, co-working, with the protagonist of our salvation, the immaculate Lamb. How did this idea of a theology of devotion come to enter Pius XII's thoughts, or those of his counsellors, on this subject? It appears to have been a reaction to those "hyper-liturgists" who, beginning in the late 1920s, took to an extreme the emphasis on the priority of the Liturgy in all its objectivity over devotions in all their possible subjectivism which was characteristic of the Benedictine school of Maria Laach. Historically, the contours of the relation between the Laacher Schule, as represented by its outstanding scholar-thinker, Dom Odo Casel, and the encyclical *Mediator Dei*, are tricky to plot. Casel and his confrères at first reacted enthusiastically to the papal letter which they hailed as the vindication of precisely that view of the Liturgy – mysteric, the action of Christ the Head in his mystical body, bringing his saving actions to bear in post-Ascension time – which they had worked to establish or re-establish in the Church. But they were soon obliged to heed other voices which declared that *Mediator Dei*, far from vindicating the monks of Laach, was precisely a condemnation of the "Rhenish innovators". As we have seen in the preceding essay, Odo Casel himself died in March 1948 before having the opportunity to clear his name, though in other respects electing the moment of his *transitus* with an impeccable sense for liturgical timing, for he expired during the Paschal vigil where he was acting as deacon, in between the proclamation *Lumen Christi!* and the singing of the *Exsultet*. An attempt to secure from the Holy Office, via the sympathetic archbishop of Salzburg, a formal statement that Casel's theology was not in view would produce only ambiguous results. At Rome, the emphasis on the unique status of liturgical prayer – a common theme of Dom Guéranger at Solesmes, the Wolter brothers at Beuron, and the Beuron daughterhouse at Laach was welcomed (we have seen the high soteriological doctrine of the Liturgy with which Pius XII opens *Mediator Dei*), but it was not intended that this emphasis should be so presented as to leave no space for the operation of a spirituality, no room for the subject's spiritual effort in a wider and so more diffuse if also more personal and to that extent more concentrated kind. Though this was not the only perilous tendency the pope saw in certain manifestations of the Liturgical Movement it is the one to which he gave the maximum critical attention.

The second chapter of the letter is devoted exclusively to the false antinomy, as Pius XII called it, between "objective" and "personal" devotion, and his insistence that subjective devotion is not only helpful but necessary if the Liturgy – including the sacraments, and above all the Mass – are to be of full effect in worshippers' lives. At Laach itself, abbot and monks rallied to the view that any contrary opinion could be ascribed to Dom Casel only by eisegesis, a reading back of them into his texts. With all due respect to Casel, without whose work much of *Mediator Dei*'s explanation of the special status of liturgical prayer would be if not unthinkable then at any rate far less readily thinkable, it must be confessed that he did occasionally provide rather large hooks on which anti-devotional interpretations of liturgical assistance could by the wrong-thinking be hung. Here he is, for instance, in his most widely read book, *Das christliche Kultmysterium*, 1932, translated into English in the year the Second Vatican Council opened. He is engaged on a comparison between prayer in the ancient Church and prayer in later Christendom, to the detriment of the latter. Prayer, he laments

> has been moving away from consciousness of the mystical body of Christ, falling into the isolated feeling and thinking of the "God-seeking" individual... The mystery itself, with its objective ordering of things according to God and real union with him, disappeared beneath a mass of more or less devotional exercises which left more freedom to individual feeling. *Devotio*, a word which to the ancients meant the Church's worship, became the devotion of a purely interior state of individual consciousness.[7]

One can easily imagine the alarm bells which unilateral interpretation of such a passage sounded in papal ears. The prospect which appalled was not that of a Mass where no one said the Rosary (the encyclical is, in fact, quite judicious in the way it exhorts pastors to encourage the fitting of such "devotions" – in the plural – to the liturgical seasons: the sorrowful mysteries during Mass at Passiontide, presumably, the glorious ones at the Masses of Easter). The prospect, rather, was of a Liturgy which could presume no devotion save that which the last celebration of the Liturgy attended had managed to generate. A Mass, in other words, at which people might well arrive as *tabulae rasae*, blackboards scrubbed clean of any evangelical writing because the wider, personal spiritual effort which the Liturgy presupposes had not been made: an absence of a due orientation signified, for instance (and these are instances the pope himself chose) by the unawareness of any need for preparation for holy communion or thanksgiving after it other than that provided by the "objective" Liturgy – the texts read out by the celebrant in the people's name, and which in the fulness of time (though this prospect was mercifully shielded from the papal gaze) could and would lead to churches where liturgies began by having to cut through cackle and on ending gave tacit signals for cackle's resumption, such that the conditions for recollectedness in approaching the eucharistic

---

[7]Odo Casel, *The Mystery of Christian Worship* (Et London 1962), p. 36.

Lord and spending time with him afterwards in prayerful union were in any case no longer met.

Pius XII's theology of devotion in *Mediator Dei* was intended to close the crack thus opening up between the celebration of the rites on the one hand and the ascetical and mystical tradition of personal prayer in the Church on the other. Basically, he takes St Thomas's teaching on what Aquinas calls the virtue of religion (that aspect of justice, our response to what is due, which governs our relations with God); links that virtue, following St Thomas, both to holiness on the one hand and to idea of devotion on the other; and applies this complex of concepts to making good the gap in the Christian approach to worship which "hyper-liturgism" had caused. Finding the origins of the word "religion" in the verb *religare*, "to bind", Aquinas had described the religious relationship as one in which we should be "bound to God as our unfailing principle", the Alpha of our lives, and "unfailingly choose him as our last end", their Omega.[8] In this sense, so Thomas goes on to explain, religion is only notionally distinct from holiness, for the word "religion" focusses attention on our taking part in cultic acts expressive of our bond with God, while the word "holiness" connotes a wider range of actions relevant to other virtues – all of which, however (and this is the capital point) have the effect of disposing us the better to divine worship.[9] In this, and here I am following the relevant section of the *Summa Theologiae* (entitled in the Cambridge translation, significantly, *Religion and Worship*) more uninterruptedly than did the pope, a special place must be given to that quality of acting Thomas calls "devotion", an attitude he defines as a willing promptness to do everything that God's service requires, caused (he goes on to explain) by contemplation of and meditation on the divine goodness and mercy, to which we are in turn moved principally by prayerful consideration of the Passion of Christ.[10] That is why, for Thomas, the chief effect of devotion

---

[8] Thomas Aquinas, *Summa Theologiae*, IIa. IIae., q.80, 1.

[9] Ibid., q.81, 8.

[10] Ibid., q. 82, 3.

is *spiritualis laetitia mentis*, "spiritual joy of mind", while its secondary effect is *tristitia secundum Deum*, a specifically divine "sadness" or "sorrow", through awareness of our own deficiencies.[11] All spiritualities in the Church, we can say, are just so many different ways of presenting and inter-relating those two fundamental kinds of pathos, Christian joy, Christian sorrow, and we can note, *en passant*, how a classical spiritual theologian like Teresa of Avila regards the sacred Liturgy as a highly congruent setting for the kind of contemplative union which, when they reach their deepest, these attitudes empower. The need to marry the objective texts and gestures of the Liturgy to ascetical and mystical effort along these lines was a salutary preoccupation of Pius XII, albeit one forced upon him, or so it would seem, by the *Mysterienkontroverse*, the debate over Maria Laach's theology of the mysteries, in inter-War German Catholicism.

It is rarely the way of the Roman church to leave historical baggage entirely behind and, once in possession of this background, we can find in Paragraphs 11 and 12 of *Sacrosanctum Concilium* reference, albeit discreet, to this disputed question in the interpretation of the Conciliar Constitution, namely, what it intends by the phrase "active" or "engaged" participation, *actuosa participatio*. What that knotty term *actuosus* means, at any rate in this section of the Constitution, is governed by the theme of the section, the necessity for "right dispositions of soul", *recti animi dispositiones*, *Sacrosanctum Concilium*'s version of the true devotion of *Mediator Dei*. "Active participation" means primarily contemplatively engaged participation, not jumping up and down, which is why section 30 of the Liturgy Constitution can include silence under this heading.

The devotion theme is, then, not so much entirely absent in *Sacrosanctum Concilium* as it is rather thoroughly submerged there. A clearer contrast between the two documents emerges when we consider the second of my claims for the relative superiority of *Mediator Dei* and that concerns the issue of the need

---

[11] Ibid., q. 82, 4.

to respect the Liturgy's previous history – and this is not so unrelated a theme to the one just investigated as might at first sight seem the case. Though *Sacrosanctum Concilium* defends the rôle in the Liturgy of what it terms "sound tradition", *sana traditio*,[12] it largely envisages a retrenchment of the Roman rite to what was, as it puts it, "in vigour in the time of the holy Fathers",[13] *ad pristinam sanctorum Patrum normam.* Just what constitutes the ending of the patristic age has never been fully determined by the Church's divines, but, once combined with the somewhat Genevan emphasis of the adjacent clauses of the Constitution on simplification of the rites (though with care not to eviscerate their substance), and the discarding of duplications or possibly superfluous late additions to the Liturgy, this reference to the period of the Fathers as providing a normative standard for liturgical reform strongly suggested to the scholars and administrators to whom the task fell of realising these recommendations in practice, that what was envisaged was not the confluence of the primitive Roman with the more florid Frankish or Gallican Liturgy of the *last* centuries of the first millennium – that synthesis which in fact produced the Roman Liturgy of the Middle Ages and the Tridentine reform, but rather the excision, wherever possible, of what did not belong to the Roman rite of the *first* centuries of that millennium.

The Liturgy Constitution of the Council, and the establishment of the *consilium* for effecting its proposals which soon followed, belong to a time when, in academic liturgiology, an ecumenical consensus reigned about the all-sufficiency of the third century Liturgy – that common "shape", as the Anglican liturgiologist Dom Gregory Dix called it, which typified all the rites, Western and Eastern, of that age. Only much more recently has the view become fashionable – it is strongly held, for instance, by Dix's fellow Anglican Paul Bradshaw, now professor of Liturgy at the University of Notre Dame, Indiana, that too much sanitisation has been carried out, both by scholars in claiming to

---

[12] *Sacrosanctum Concilium*, 23.
[13] Ibid., 50.

detect in very disparate materials a primitive common form, and, what is more to our purposes, by liturgical reformers in attempting to prune away whatever is particular in the growth of the Liturgy in this rite or that in later time.

The relevance of this to the devotion theme should become clear if I may be allowed to cite at this juncture an encomium of the historic Dominican rite made by the liturgical historian William Bonniwell some two years before *Mediator Dei*. Praising the mid-thirteenth century revision of that rite by Humbert of Romans as "a masterpiece surpassed by no other rite in the Latin church", Bonniwell explained that he was speaking in terms of the goal set by the developed Western liturgy of the high Middle Ages:

> the ancient Roman qualities of simplicity, dignity and practicality enriched by a warmer devotion and by a restrained dramatic element so appealing to human nature...[14]

The stripping away of various ceremonies and the more devotional non-Roman prayers as unnecessary post-patristic accretions undermined the capacity of the reformed Roman Liturgy to sustain that devotional atmosphere which was needed if the "right dispositions of soul" desiderated by the Constitution were to endure – never mind to be brought more fully into play. Exactly such truncation of the Liturgy was what *Mediator Dei*, noting that the early Fathers had no exclusive monopoly on the best tunes, had tried to prevent. Stigmatising the desire for such drastic pruning as the consequence of "archaeologism", the pope warned that while

> to go back in mind and heart to the sources of the sacred liturgy is wise and praiseworthy, ... the desire to restore everything indiscriminately to its ancient condition is neither
> ...[15]

And the reason is that, just as with the development of doctrine, a Catholic Christian does not maintain that divine guidance left the Church to her own devices after the death of the last of the

---

[14] W. R. Bonniwell, O. P., *A History of the Dominican Liturgy, 1215-1945* (New York 1945), p.193. Italics added.

[15] *Mediator Dei*, 65.

Fathers, so here too, the post-patristic evolution of the Liturgy cannot be regarded as outside God's Providence, cannot be written off as certainly not the result of divine grace working on the corporate imagination of the Church. The attempt of so highly placed a Roman liturgist today as Dom Adrien Nocent to take to a logical conclusion the "de-mediaevalisation" (to coin an ugly phrase) of the Roman rite undertaken by the post-Conciliar consilium through abolishing such remaining elements of post-patristic practice as the elevation, after the Consecration, of Host and chalice, shows how deeply rooted is a prejudice in matters of the Liturgy which, were it transferred to the field of doctrine, would immediately identify one as un-Catholic in a fundamental sense.[16]

Let us now tip the scales a little the other way as I move on to my third principal disparity of theological substance in this tale of two documents – this time to the credit of *Sacrosanctum Concilium*, rather than *Mediator Dei*. The question of the unique ontological status of the Liturgy is the question of what befalls the prayers we use in church – prayers, most of them, not directly biblical in origin and so the result, primarily, of human creativity rather than divine inspiration (we do not say of them as we say of the Scriptures, *Verbum Domini*, "This is the Word of the Lord") – when we deploy those prayers in a strictly liturgical fashion. In what way is the standing of those prayers altered? The answer of *Mediator Dei* is that these prayers are taken up into the relation which, since the time of Christ's saving historical acts, holds good between the Church, his mystical body, and himself, the Church's head, and consequently, since he is in his own person the God-man, the divine-human mediator, into that eternally actual dialogue which unites the Son with the Father. As the pope put it:

> The sacred liturgy is ... the public worship which our
> Redeemer, the Head of the Church, offers to the heavenly

---

[16] A. Nocent, *A Re-reading of the Renewed Liturgy* (Collegeville, Minn., 1994); some more comments on this in my *Looking at Liturgy: A Critical View of its Contemporary Form* (San Francisco 1996), pp. 116-118.

184

Father and which the community of Christ's faithful pays to its Founder, and through him, to the eternal Father; briefly, it is the whole public worship of the Mystical Body of Jesus Christ, Head and members.[17]

This is why the Liturgy has such dignity, significance, efficacy, why it is, precisely, the *sacred* Liturgy. Pius XII had gone on record, in the encyclical, as singling out the special debt of the universal Church to that understanding of the Liturgy pioneered by the revived Benedictinism of the nineteenth and twentieth centuries (what he called "the devoted zeal of certain monasteries of the renowned Benedictine Order"[18]), and if we were to look for the theological sources of his ontology of the Liturgy we need search no further than the Solesmes of Guéranger on the one hand, and the Maria Laach of Casel (to whom, as I have stressed, the encyclical has a complex relation of attraction and repulsion), on the other. Here, for instance is Guéranger in the general preface to the *Année liturgique*:

> Jesus Christ himself is ... the means as well as the object of the Liturgy, and that is why the "Year of the Church" we propose to set forth in this work is nothing other than the manifestation of Jesus Christ and of his mysteries in the Church and in the faithful soul ... If each year the Church renews her youth "like the eagle's", this is because, through the liturgical cycle, she is visited by her Spouse according to the proportion of her needs. Each year she sees him an infant in the crib, fasting on the mountain, offering himself on the Cross rising again from the tomb, founding his Church and instituting his sacraments, ascending once more to the Father's right, sending out his Spirit to men; and the graces of these divine mysteries are in turn renewed in the Church in such a fashion that, rendered fertile as need suggests, the garden of the Church sends up to her Spouse at all times [here Guéranger cites the *Song of Solomon*] "by the breath of the

---

[17] Ibid., 24.
[18] Ibid., 5.

North Wind and the South the sweet fragrance of her perfumes".[19]

Pius XII's formulation of the relation between the Liturgy and Christ in his mysteries actually rises beyond this, however, in section 176 of *Mediator Dei* where the pope speaks, in terms more redolent of Casel, of the liturgical year as being in its inmost reality *Christus ipse, qui in sua Ecclesia perseverat,* "Christ himself, living on in his Church", so that human beings may encounter his mysteries – and not just, we may gloss the text as saying, their fruits or the graces that flow from them, for we are to encounter them as they are in themselves and *per eadem quodammodo viverent,* "in a certain sense live by means of them". For what is this save Casel's view that the Liturgy in its total unfolding in the Church's year makes present not just the effects of Christ's redeeming work – from Annunciation to Glorification – but Christ himself *in* those redemptive actions still as fully actual as they ever were in history yet given to human beings again – indeed, again and again – *sacramentally*, through the mediation of sacred signs.

But the Liturgy, for pope Pius, as for Guéranger at Solesmes, and Casel at Laach (and here we might usefully note a third possible Benedictine source mid-way, in time and space, between these two – Dom Columba Marmion at Maredsous), is the rendering actual in present time of a *past* reality – albeit one that, because of its unique divine-human quality is not simply past but held in God's eternity. There is little or nothing in *Mediator Dei* about the Liturgy not as Christological remembrance but as Christological anticipation of *a future yet to come* – the principal reason no doubt why the encyclical's theology of the Advent season is so disappointingly moralistic and jejune.[20] And here is where *Sacrosanctum Concilium* helpfully enters in, to complete the picture.

---

[19] Prosper Guéranger, "Préface générale", *L'Année liturgique. Avent* (Tours 1920), p. xix, citing *Song of Solomon* 4, 17.
[20] *Mediator Dei*, 165.

> In the earthly liturgy [declare the Fathers of Vatican II] we
> take part in a foretaste of that heavenly liturgy which is
> celebrated in the holy city of Jerusalem towards which we
> journey as pilgrims ... ; we eagerly await our Saviour, the Lord
> Jesus Christ, until he, our life, shall appear, and we too will
> appear with him in glory.[21]

The reference to the Parousia is not highly developed, but, given
the concision of the theological summaries in the Liturgy
Constitution no more can it be overlooked. Jean Corbon, who
lives in the Centre des Dominicains at Beirut in the Lebanon and
was selected to write the book on prayer in the new *Catechism*,
produced in 1980 a theology of the Liturgy, in French, *Liturgie de
Source*, ably translated into our language in 1988 as *The Wellspring
of Worship*, which can fairly be described as a sustained
commentary on this eighth section of the Second Vatican
Council's liturgical charter. The great thing about Corbon's
presentation of future eschatology in *Liturgie de Source* is that he
does not, as can so easily happen, set it over against the realised
eschatology represented by *Mediator Dei* and the Benedictine
doctors. It is as he puts it

> because we are "already" in the eternal liturgy that its current
> carries us the more impatiently to its consummation...[22]

citing the way that, in the Johannine Apocalypse, the prayer of the
martyrs beneath the heavenly altar is precisely, How long?, how
long before the Parousia come upon us for which the Spirit and
the Bride call "Come!". And that understanding perfectly reflects
the understanding of the bishops in *Sacrosanctum Concilium*: it is
because the earthly Liturgy is even now the breakthrough of the
heavenly (realised eschatology) that the Church is propelled
towards her definitive encounter in history with the returning
Lord, anticipating in her worship (future eschatology) that
glorious consummation of all things.

Let me now in short measure register for the sake of
completeness two final points of contrast and comparison between

---

[21] *Sacrosanctum Concilium*, 8.
[22] Jean Corbon, *The Wellspring of Worship*, op. cit., p. 42.

Mediator Dei and *Sacrosanctum Concilium* before bringing to an end this "tale of two documents" by asking what light it throws on how we should evaluate the revolutionary period. through which we have passed, that question of Dickens – was it the best of times, or the worst?

First, we could note with interest the way the Liturgy Constitution echoes *Mediator Dei*'s warning against "undue fondness for innovation" by its own insistence that interventions in the Liturgy's organic growth should only be made when some imperative need of the Church commands – though in fact *Sacrosanctum Concilium*'s licence to national liturgical commissions to propose pastoral adaptations turned out to be a blank cheque of the kind known to no bank, for this one can be perpetually re-presented![23] Important too is the manner in which *Mediator Dei* directly affirms the primarily latreutic character of the Liturgy, its theocentric nature, while *Sacrosanctum Concilium* makes the same point only concessively:

> *Although* the sacred liturgy is above all things the worship of the divine Majesty, it nevertheless contains much instruction for the faithful.[24]

A nuance? Possibly, but if so then, evidently, an infectious one. The Liturgy Constitution looked to liturgical reform as a means to create a better instructed laity: not at all an ignoble objective but, in the light of *Mediator Dei*, an example of using the wrong tool. For the papal letter, too, the purpose of the sacred Liturgy is to form in us that mind which was in Christ Jesus, but, as Pius XII explains, what this means in the context of worship is above all the formation in us of those attitudes with which our Great High Priest went to the offering of his saving Sacrifice to the heavenly Father insofar as redeemed creatures, who are not and never will be the Redeemer, can make those movements in the Heart of Christ their own.

---

[23] *Mediator Dei*, 7; *Sacrosanctum Concilium*, 23.

[24] *Sacrosanctum Concilium* 33 (emphasis added); cf. especially *Mediator Dei* 75-79, but also *passim*.

So *was* it, then, the worst of times, rather than the best? As I suggested, the Great Revolution of the West is not the weakest analogy we can take for the effects – like those of the Revolution, in large part unintended – of the Second Vatican Council. Dickens, in the thoughts he suggested for Sydney Carton on his way to the guillotine, recommended one kind of answer. That answer is not a fine calculation of "pros" and "cons" which, in the nature of things, our limited grasp of the ways of divine Providence makes us ill-equipped to make. Nor would so nice an answer stir up in us the spiritual re-conversion response to the Lord of history requires. What Dickens would elicit from his readers is a hope for the future based on a readiness to learn the hard lessons of the present and also (since the deficiencies of one age are never entirely self-bred, they come with a genealogy) of the past.

> I see [so Dickens allowed Carton to prophesy] a beautiful city and a brilliant people rising from this abyss, and, in their struggles to be truly free, in their triumphs and defeats, through long, long years to come, I see the evil of this time and of the previous time of which this is the natural birth, gradually making expiation for itself and wearing out.[25]

If it is true, as Newman claimed, that the Church constantly dies and rises again through history in imitation of her Master and Lord, how could that "slumber" and "restoration" of which the *Essay on the Development of Christian Doctrine* not have its counterpart in matters of the Liturgy of the Church?[26] That renaissance to which we look forward will include, I venture to suggest, the recovery of the liturgical, married with devotionalism, of *Mediator Dei*, but also *Sacrosanctum Concilium*'s looking beyond the Church here and now to the final Church arrayed in the glorious garments of the redeemed when Christ comes with all his saints.

---

[25] Charles Dickens, *A Tale of Two Cities*, III. 15.
[26] John Henry Newman, *Essay on the Development of Christian Doctrine: The Edition of 1845* (Harmondsworth 1974), p. 448.

Today there are not lacking commentators who, observing the present difficulties of the Church of Rome and its steady retreat in societies where its worship once formed the framework for living, take up the rôle, in Dickens' novel, of the knitting-women – ghoulish attendants at a death scene as the "crashing engine" (the guillotine) "constantly whirrs up and falls". Those macabre assistants fail to reckon with the force of words from the Gospel according to St John which Carton cites and which underlie Newman's account of the dying and rising Church of the mysteries:

> I am the Resurrection and the Life, saith the Lord, he that believeth in me, though he were dead, yet shall he live: and whosoever liveth and believeth in me, shall never die.[27]

---

[27] John 11, 25-26, cited ibid.

X

HYMNS ANCIENT AND POSTMODERN:

CATHERINE PICKSTOCK'S
AFTER WRITING

Catherine Pickstock's *After Writing*, described as a treatise "on the liturgical consummation of philosophy", is an extraordinary book which can be read in at least three ways: as an assault on that Protean phenomenon postmodernism (but more specifically in the form given it by the French philosopher and literary theorist Jacques Derrida); as an account of the decline of authentic ontology – that is, faithful thinking about *being* – in the culture of the West; and as a defense of the traditional Roman Catholic liturgy (which she, as an Anglican, prefers to call the mediaeval Western rite), a defense couched in philosophically sophisticated as well as (often) poetically lyrical terms. Although these three aspects of *After Writing: On the Liturgical Consummation of Philosophy*[1] are by no means kept in hermetically sealed compartments (that is why each of them can provide a total reading of Dr. Pickstock's study), they also can be said to unfold in a sequence.

Thus first, in the book's opening chapter introducing an account of what the author terms the "polity of death," it is the challenge to Derrida's postmodernism that predominates, though the ontological and liturgical themes are delicately indicated in references to Platonic metaphysics and to "doxology," the glorifying of the divine. Then, secondly, in chapters two and three and in a lengthy section entitled "Transition," we are invited to consider how a human community that, in its forms of thought and speech, lay open to transcendence (as the city of Socrates lay)

---

[1] C. Pickstock, *After Writing: On the Liturgical Consummation of Philosophy* (Oxford 1998).

became, rather, spiritually cramped and self-enclosed to the detriment of the human person, and how this process was accompanied by a falling into oblivion of the mystery of being, which alone makes the good possible in its full flourishing, such that we now face, in postmodernism, a fundamentally nihilistic reading of the world. In this sad history, Pickstock hints, defective attitudes to the Holy Eucharist, the central religious symbol of Greco-Roman civilization in its Christian development, played a hitherto unsuspected part. Finally, in the last four chapters of the book, "The Sacred Polis," in a sympathetic reading of the classical Roman liturgy, Pickstock claims to show how that *ensemble* of words and gestures at the heart of the worshipping life of mediaeval Christendom consummates the philosophical intimations of Socrates, safeguards a spiritually spacious human city, sustains a true ontology where creation is an ever-renewed gift from the unspeakable Source we call God, and – not least – answers far more satisfactorily than postmodernists the questions the postmodernists themselves have posed.

In this essay, I shall look in turn at these three inter-connected emphases of *After Writing*: anti-postmodernism;[2] criticism of the later Western metaphysics and epistemology in their cultural context; and the case for the Liturgy – or at any rate for the traditional Roman rite – as, in the book's daring sub-title, the "Consummation of Philosophy."

First, then, what does Pickstock have to say about postmodernism? Actually, many readers will want a prior question answered, namely, What *is* postmodernism? – for the author, presuming our acquaintance with this elusive body of thought that is more influential in departments of literature than among philosophers themselves, drops us to fend for ourselves *in medias res*. Looking around for a brief *précis* of Derrida's thought that might contextualize usefully her discussion, I found the following

---

[2] At a Cambridge *Communio* Circle meeting of 23 May 1998 where Dr. Pickstock's book was discussed, she emphasized that she welcomed postmodernism's dismantling of attempts at full determination of the real in previous philosophy – but not its doing so in favor of nihilism rather than of openness to divine plenitude.

summary in a spirited account by another woman writer, the American, Charlene Spretnak, who, though a feminist who has abandoned Catholic Christianity for a personal syncretism, shares Pickstock's view that, *au fond*, postmodernism is a manipulative Nominalism that leads straight into nihilism by its love-affair with what Spretnak calls "extreme groundlessness."[3] She writes:

> In building on the structural theory of language proposed by Ferdinand de Saussure – that meaning is produced by the difference between "signifiers" (words, which have an arbitrary but fixed connection with the "signified") in the language chain – Derrida maintains that every word is divided into a phonic "signifier" and a mental "signified" and that language is a system of *différance* (from the verb meaning both to differ and to defer) between these two phenomena, not a system of independently meaningful units. His term for what he perceives as the fallacy of the self-presentation of meaning or presence is *logocentrism*, which represses the "lag" of *différance* inherent in the act of using phonic "signifiers" (words) to express mental "signifieds" (ideas, concepts, perceptions, or emotions). Moreover, Derrida denies that "signifiers" can have any fixed meaning since the meaning of a word or concept occurs only in a specific context ("textual location") every time it is used.

And Spretnak goes on to explain that

> We, of course, can never know the precise mental context in which a writer uses a word, but her or his intention is not important anyway, according to Derrida, since all language is merely self-referential, a chain of signifiers referring to other signifiers so that language is always indeterminate. Hence, he concludes, meaning and consciousness do not exist outside language; all meaning is temporary and relative; and there can be no central, original, or transcendental signifier (for example, God, History, Man, Reason) outside the invented language system of differences, which determine our only possible means of thought.[4]

---

[3] C. Spretnak, *States of Grace: The Recovery of Meaning in the Postmodern Age* (San Francisco 1993), p. 239
[4] Ibid., p. 234.

It is noteworthy that, starting from so different a departure-point from Pickstock's, Charlene Spretnak hits upon a number of the same themes in her critique of Derrida – autonomy from relationship, separateness, control through abstraction, disdain for mere bodies in the insistence that everything is already a "supplemented" entity shaped in cultural perceptions,[5] and the paradox that a theory that champions difference, multiplicity and "centrelessness" is itself "totalizing" in its dismissal of all other perceptions of reality. "'Detachment' and 'shallow engagement' follow."[6] The gap – indeed abyss – that separates the interpretative schemes in which the selfsame criticisms of postmodernism appear, is, however, unmistakable. It derives not only from Catherine Pickstock's *pietas* towards Plato, whose thought for Spretnak is an egregious example of the male's obsession with "transcendence beyond the body," but, even more profoundly, from the dependence of Pickstock's thinking on Christian revelation as construed in the light, above all, of the Liturgy: *prima theologia*, "prime theology," as the American Benedictine liturgiologist Aidan Kavanaugh has called it.[7]

Pickstock's own deconstruction of Derrida turns crucially on the latter's reading of Plato's dialogue the *Phaedrus*. This is a dialogue of Plato's middle period which more conventional students of classical literature would describe as about either the philosophical possibilities of rhetoric or about *eros*, that love which is at once desire for the pleasure that comes from the beautiful and self-commitment to the good, or again – for the staid but careful Cambridge commentary by Reginald Hackforth – both of these at once.[8] Derrida, in an influential essay, "Plato's Pharmacy," used *his* version of this dialogue as a vehicle for his own deconstructionism, and Pickstock sets out to show that in so doing he understood neither Plato nor the implications of his own proposals.

---

[5] "Our bodies being mere docile recipients of various power-laden 'discourses' and diffuse practices of cultural discipline and self-discipline..." (ibid., p. 124).

[6] Ibid., p. 238.

[7] A. Kavanaugh, O.S.B., *On Liturgical Theology* (New York 1984).

[8] R. Hackforth, trans., *Plato's Phaedrus* (Cambridge 1952; 1972), pp. 8–11.

The rhetoric whose philosophical value Socrates debates in the *Phaedrus* can be either persuasive writing or persuasive speech, but whereas Derrida grants primacy to the written word, which lends itself better to his analysis of language in general (language is a constantly re-interpreted commentary on itself, just as texts refer to other texts and generate fresh texts in their interpretation), Socrates, and Pickstock after him, give the palm to living speech. For them, the written text, easily manipulated by plausible transfer to other contexts – sophistry, in fact – is philosophically far less suggestive than the kind of speaking commended and exemplified by Socrates in the dialogue. Much better, then, is a sowing of the living word in another's soul – though of course oral communication *can* take the form of a *false* rhetoric. As Hackforth puts it,

> The way of the true rhetoric is difficult and laborious, but its justification is that in seeking the truth we are seeking to do the pleasure of the gods.[9]

Catherine Pickstock's account of the *Phaedrus* aims to draw out the full significance of that latter remark for a discourse that is indeed full of gods – local divinities who inspire Socrates in the riverside setting where the dialogue takes place, and Eros, the god of love, who elsewhere in Plato's writing tends to be treated as merely an intermediary, a *daimon*. By no mere formal protocol, in her view, does the dialogue end with Socrates' prayer to Pan – and with allusion to the social context, the place in the *polis*, of that prayer, when Phaedrus himself adds his own final remark, "Make it a prayer for me too, since friends have all things in common."[10]

If this liturgical *mise-en-scène* of the *Phaedrus* is altogether absent from Derrida's account, there are many other respects in which Pickstock's reading of the dialogue differs *toto caelo* from his. First, and closely connected with this, for Catherine Pickstock, the human subject in Plato, not least here, is less a rational contemplator of abstract ideas than he is a "doxologist," a liturgical

---

[9] Ibid., p. 152.
[10] *Phaedrus*, 279C.

praiser of the divine. For this epistemology, the seer is certainly "linked" to the seen, but the subject does not claim to master the object, since what Pickstock calls "doxological distance,"[11] a self-abasing wonderment about reality typical of a city open to the gods, always intervenes.[12]

Secondly, the written text, which is more obviously an artefact extended in space than it is an act carried out in time, becomes, if it be erected into an ideal of language as in Derrida's notion of textuality, a means of shrugging off such inconvenient dimensions of human life as its temporal and contingent qualities – qualities which (as we shall see) are in fact hallmarks of the giftedness of existence: of what, in the light of Judeo-Christian revelation, will come to be called "creation." Ideologically to exalt the written word over the spoken – as Derrida thinks Plato's Socrates ought to have exalted it – is, despite all postmodern protestations of *vive la différance*, effectively to attempt a homogenization of human relations, which would eliminate the *play* of speech. To insist that truth and value are never really present, even via a text, but are always indefinitely (in a favored term of Derrida's) "postponed," is to fall victim to the fear – a really crippling fear for human living – that one will never recover one's investment in any object. So better not to invest at all. For Plato, who has grasped the authentic notion of transcendence, the Good (and the Form of the Good is for Plato ultimate reality) makes its presence felt through the gifts it bestows, "giv[ing] things to be seen" as Pickstock puts it in a witty re-formulation of Plato's comparison of the transcendent Good with the light of the sun. And like the landscapes which the daily rising of the sun reveals to us, the good always "arrives through time,"[13] as through the contingencies of our experience of good and beautiful persons and things we come to participate in goodness and beauty themselves, the two being interconnected insofar as the beautiful is the shining forth of the radiance of the good.

---

[11] C. Pickstock, *After Writing*, p. 7.
[12] Cf. the account of the "Socratic gaze," ibid. , pp. 32–33.
[13] Ibid., p. 13.

Thirdly, all this takes place in a religiously sensitive city – for to speak of how, through finite signs, what Plato terms a "memory" of the primal Good is triggered in our souls requires recourse to the tradition of human mythmaking. Mythopeic images take over in Plato from the point where rational argument has no more to say, but they do so by following the *direction* that rationality has indicated. As Pickstock puts it, the good is not "available to a Cartesian measuring gaze."[14] What Socrates is commending in the *Phaedrus* is

> not a retreat into an inviolable self, but rather an opening of the self – to receive the mediation of the transcendent in and through the immanent.[15]

That interpretation of Platonic memory is powerfully assisted by Socrates' view of the true *eros*, which makes us go out of ourselves towards some finite presentation of the good. Contrary to Derrida's fears, the Platonist is always essentially *in communion with* other beings.

> So, contrary to Derrida's claim that Platonic metaphysics is to be found in a privileging of truth-as-presence, and of subjectivity as interiority, it seems that from the enumeration of the myriad stimuli in which the philosopher-lover is immersed, one should derive instead an account of the self as constituted by its opening to receive its environment, both physical and divine.[16]

How different from Derrida's subject, whose speech-acts are determined in advance by the texts through which writing acts upon him, and who in this scene has violence done to him. In striking contrast is the participatory subject of Plato, above all in the liturgical setting where through hymns (it is hymnographic poets that Plato is happiest to see in his city) one praises what is worthy of praise by a doxological expression which renders one truly "centred" – Pickstock's word for a just notion of personal

---

[14] Ibid., p. 21.
[15] Ibid., p. 25.
[16] Ibid., p. 32.

identity.[17] By doxology, persons – otherwise elusive, constructed as they seem by social roles and masks – are constituted ontologically in their proper density for the first time. Doxology, Pickstock suggests by a rhetorical question, "is the gift of humanity itself, ordered through song and dance."[18] She does not have much to say about the significance of sacred dance as an identification of our place in the cosmic dance of the gods or, Christianized, the angels (here a richly documented study by James Miller on this theme, cunningly entitled *Measures of Wisdom*, could have strengthened her case):[19] the doxological ethos is spread abroad, in her focus of attention, by liturgical *speech*.

We come now to Catherine Pickstock's account of how the Platonic city, where speech, reflection, and life are doxological in orientation and therefore, as her concluding chapters will suggest, uniquely fitted to be a *praeparatio evangelica*, was in fact deserted by those who should have been its defenders in the Christian (though also post-Christian) history of the West. Thirty years before *After Writing*, the American Jesuit Walter Ong, cited there in his capacity as author of a major study on Peter Ramus,[20] the fiercely anti-Aristotelian sixteenth century logician, argued a case in book-length form that oral-aural man – man as the bearer and the hearer of living speech – has fought a losing battle first against chirographic man – man as script-maker – and then, much more seriously (for manuscripts, owing to the tediousness and cost of their production, belong to what is perforce a *predominantly* oral culture) against typographic man – man the maker of print, and of the electronic extensions of print made possible by advanced technology, such that now people think of language as essentially writing, and therefore laid out in space, despite the fact that

---

[17] Ibid., p. 39.

[18] Ibid., p. 40.

[19] J. Miller, *Measures of Wisdom: The Cosmic Dance in Classical and Christian Antiquity* (Toronto 1986).

[20] Pierre de la Ramée, 1515–1572. On whom see W. Ong, S.J., *Ramus, Method, and the Decay of Dialogue* (Cambridge, Mass. 1958).

language is really primarily sound, and therefore an event in time.[21] In his study, Ong anticipates some of Pickstock's favored vocabulary and themes in her version of *der Untergang des Abendlandes*, "the decline of the West." Thus Ong, like Pickstock, regrets

> the tendency of the past few centuries to overspatialize the universe so that everything is reduced to models picturable in space, and what is unpicturable ("unimaginable" is often the term invoked) is discarded as impossible or unreal.[22]

The demotion of orality, living speech, opens a door to the advent of faulty epistemologies and erroneous metaphysics – a notion taken much further, and with more sustained exploration of the history of philosophy in Pickstock's book. In proto-Pickstockian vein, Ong laments that, as intellectual culture forsakes the oral, it comes to treat words not as celebrations but as tools, while the wider culture rapidly replaces memory by records. But records are external aids to recalling, not actual remembrance.[23]

Moreover, according to Ong, in a fashion highly relevant to Pickstock, a new and confining kind of literalism comes to reign. In his words,

> An alphabetic culture, which puts a premium on visualist qualities such as sharp outline and clear-cut sequence, is likely to regard the literal meaning, in the sense of plain or definite meaning, as something altogether wholesome and altogether desirable, and to regard other remote, perhaps more profoundly symbolic, meanings with disfavour.[24]

Closure to deep meaning where texts are concerned is paralleled, so Ong tells us, by concentration on physical extension in scanning the extra-textual world, and this is aided and abetted by theories of knowledge which "thingify" human beings by treating them as "phenomena," a concealed visual metaphor, whereas in

---

[21] W. Ong, S. J. , *The Presence of the Word: Some Prolegomena for Cultural and Religious History* (New Haven and London 1967).

[22] Ibid., p. 7.

[23] Ibid., 23.

[24] Ibid., p. 47.

reality persons are in mutual communication as interiors through the resonant sounding box of speech.

Though Ong does not use the term "nihilism," or relate the trends he is describing, as Catherine Pickstock does, to the social and economic order, he considers that the passing of oral-aural cultures with their tendency to treat actuality as "united in some kind of harmony" is linked both to disengagement from wider reality and to the development of individualism. As he puts it:

> Since pure interiors (persons) do communicate with one another so largely by voice, the silencing of words portends in some way withdrawal into oneself. Such withdrawal need not be antisocial, for the interior into which one withdraws is the ground of all communication. Religious silence, for example, undertaken in union with others and out of regard for God and all mankind, can be fruitful and is, but such silence relates at many points to the spoken word and constitutes itself a kind of communication or encounter. So does writing, of course. And yet, because it consists of silent words, writing introduces a whole new set of structures within the psyche: communication which lacks the normal social aspect of communication, encounter with the one who is not present, participation in the thought of others without commitment or involvement. Oral or illiterate peoples are understandably suspicious of literates as "slickers," the noncommitted and disinterested whom one cannot trust.[25]

And like Pickstock again, Ong regards the disprizing of orality as key to de-sacralization or, if one prefers, the secularization of culture. In a final citation:

> The shift of focus from the spoken word and habits of auditory synthesis to the alphabetized written word and visual synthesis (actuality is measured by picturability) devitalizes the universe, weakens the sense of presence in man's life-world, and in doing so tends to render this world profane, to make it an agglomeration of things.[26]

I have lingered on these similarities between Ong and Pickstock for three reasons. First, it should create confidence in

---

[25] Ibid., p. 126.
[26] Ibid., p. 162.

her analysis of the decline of the sacred polis that her conclusions are anticipated by a scholar who, for all his commendation of commitment, is a good deal cooler in tone (his study is presented as a contribution to the history of changes in the psychological organization of the "*sensorium*" – our senses considered as a unity that can be co-ordinated in various ways – and the effects of this on culture). In particular, it may reassure those readers who are anxious that Pickstock may have caught from her postmodernist sources and adversaries that disease which Anthony Quinton terms "hypernegation":

> the florid inflation by which these...philosophers cannot deny a partial falsehood without asserting the absolute, hyperbolic truth of its opposite.[27]

Secondly, Ong confirms that a constellation of issues revolving around the conflicting claims to primacy of speech and writing – notions of presence and personhood, representations of reality as conceivable only if picturable (that is, convertible into diagram), and the replacement of rhetoric and disputation by a private dialectic of philosophical method, executed, as in the case of Descartes, within the individual's head – has something to do, and perhaps a great deal to do, with the plausibility or otherwise of belief in God. For Ong, restoration of the primacy of orality in culture does not, of course, by itself re-actualize revelation and render God's Word newly audible. But it would prepare the way for such an encounter.

Thirdly, however, the similarities I have traced in the work of these two thinkers make the dissimilarities of their prescriptions stand out in greater relief. For Ong, the advent of such new audial media as telephone, radio, and, in its sound aspect, television, is already ushering in a new era of hopefulness for a religion of the living word (evidently, he did not foresee the alternative epiphanies of personal computers, e-mail, and the Internet!). Though he mentions the Liturgy in a passing aside ("The Roman and Greek liturgies made classical rhetoric a tremendously effective

---

[27] J. O'Grady, reviewing A. Quinton, *From Wodehouse to Wittgenstein* (London 1998), in *The Spectator* 280.8859 (25 May 1998), p. 34.

vehicle for biblical teaching"),[28] it does not occur to him that the possible recovery of oral primacy, if contextualized in a new understanding of the doxological dimension of speech, would give the traditional liturgies of Christendom a crucial pertinence. If in this he is manifesting the customary Jesuit *insouciance*, honorable exceptions aside, towards the liturgical, he also, in his concern for a Catholic appreciation of Scripture, does fuller justice to the role of the Bible in the transmission of revelation than does Catherine Pickstock: a subsidiary but significant theme of *The Presence of the Word* is what he terms "the massive oral underpinnings of the Bible."[29]

It is the use Pickstock makes of the historic Roman rite, and the concomitant idea of eucharistic "Real Presence" which must finally detain us, but before reaching that concluding section of this presentation, I must do more justice, however briefly, to the specifically Pickstockian account of Western apostasy, the coming of the "over-spatialized" (in a sense which by now should be clear) city of "immanentist modernity," which is for her at the same time a necropolis, or "city of death."

Absent from Ong – who, despite his pre-conciliar Jesuit formation (his book was originally lectures given at Yale in 1964), shows little interest in the varieties of Christian Scholasticism – is John Duns Scotus, a key figure in the rogues' gallery in *After Writing*. The Scotist doctrine, formulated in opposition to Aquinas, of the univocity of being (to be is for everything – from God to an amoeba – one and the same), by rendering being graspable, deprives it of the mystery which belongs to it as a many-splendored gift, whose giving is mediated by time and contingency, and it sunders being from its plenary divine Source – and, moreover, prepares the way for the reduction of being to the grasp of the Cartesian *cogito*, itself operating, so Catherine Pickstock holds, by reference to a view of the real as a city laid out according to a grid. "The given," she remarks by way of summing up, "is no longer in excess of what can be known by means of

---

[28] W. Ong, S.J., *The Presence of the Word*, p. 212.

[29] Ibid. , p. 21.

method";[30] and this is now as true of the subject, the knowing agent, as it is of being, what the knowing agent should explore.

Also not found in the Jesuit scholar is Pickstock's suggestion that the triumph of writing and the epistemological and metaphysical consequences this brings in its train, especially when the way is prepared by faulty ontology of a Scotist sort, can be seen working itself out in practice in such different settings as the early modern scientific community and the architecture of the Baroque. For what is the science of the late seventeenth century Royal Society if not the apotheosis of ideas of experimental repeatability, observation, and material visibility associated with the written; and what is Baroque building if not a theatrical exploitation of space at the behest of an absolute monarch, the political counterpart of the clarity and distinctness in organizing ideas commanded by the solitary Cartesian "I"? These suggestions, expressed at times in language which Dr. Sheridan Gilley in a study of Catholic counter-culturalism has called "passionate unintelligibility," are thought-provoking without necessarily being convincing. It is, surely, the positivistic interpretation of early modern scientific method that is objectionable, rather than the method *per se* (what natural science could dispense with the features to which Pickstock objects?). Indeed, more sympathetic readings of the Baroque might be offered. Thus, for instance, J.R. Martin, in his Penguin textbook on the Baroque, says of the *Cathedra Petri*, in its setting among statues of the Church Fathers below Bernini's so-called *Gloria* (a "rendering in bronze and stucco of the heavenly host that now encompasses the oval west window of the basilica [of St. Peter's] around the dove [of the Holy Spirit] in stained glass"):[31]

> these monumental and imposing forms, which thrust themselves so emphatically upon our senses, are understood to owe their existence to the spiritual light, of which they are, so to speak, mere concretions.[32]

---

[30] *After Writing*, p. 65.

[31] C. Avery, *Bernini: Genius of the Baroque* (London 1997), p. 110.

[32] J.R. Martin, *Baroque* (Harmondsworth 1977; 1991), p. 234.

And in this, the Baroque church-building exemplifies what Evelyn Waugh called the "positive achievement" of the "great open altar, where Mass is said in a flood of light," a "triumph of light over darkness consciously realized"[33]; the light in question being not simply the light of reason – Christianly acceptable though this is where it remains that of a rationality open to transcendence – but the pneumatic light deriving, as Bernini's Roman altar-piece suggests, from *gracious* illumination by the Holy Spirit. And yet, the notion that Baroque carnival may be an over-compensation for the formalism of post-Cartesian philosophy and the semantic poverty of the developing scientific discourse seems not altogether unpersuasive.

Introducing us to our final topic, Catherine Pickstock's account of the Liturgy itself, is her last motif under the heading of the "spatialized city": the emergence of a simplified grammar for written speech, with a preponderance of one clause sentences abounding in nouns, suited to the transmission of informational data, typical of, say, modern written English, and at the antipodes from what, historically, liturgical language has sounded like. Thus, everything is in place for a city of death, evoked most graphically in Derrida's philosophy, for which only death itself can guarantee the singularity of identity that otherwise eludes the text-constructed self, and alone is *my* possession which *I* can offer.[34]

It follows from Catherine Pickstock's genealogy of our woes that reversing these developments entails recovering a doxological voice – which in the context of Christian theology means a *liturgic* voice above all. There are few better ways to find out people's liturgical tastes and convictions than to ask them when they think the golden age of the Liturgy ended. Answers are available on a spectrum ranging from the first Sunday before the opening of the first session of the Second Vatican Council at one end to the Last Supper at the other. Catherine Pickstock also has her place in this scheme. The late Middle Ages are described as the time when

---

[33]E. Waugh, "A Coronation in 1930," in *When the Going was Good* (London 1946; Harmondsworth 1951), pp. 129–30.
[34] *After Writing*, p. 111.

a liturgical ordering of society was giving way to an organization in terms of the exercise of pure will and divorced from love, combined with a formalized logic and an increased enforcement of positive law.[35]

Though entering the important caveat that the notion of a truly liturgically ordered society in the High Middle Ages may not have been actually realized, since the more fundamental claim is that "certain social and intellectual conditions of possibility for such an order were present" then,[36] Pickstock follows the French exponent of *nouvelle théologie* Henri de Lubac in her view that in late mediaeval practice, by contrast with earlier, the Western liturgy lost that sense of how it is the Eucharist that makes the Church. Christ's sacramental body generates in the Mass his mystical body, the true sacred city of a people defined by their relation to the unique historical body of Jesus Christ. As she writes:

> This manifestation in time of the effects of the historical body of Jesus in the communion of the Church and the sacrament opened the space of liturgy as the "site" where the visible community . . . and the mysterious work . . . combined, sustaining the linear series extending from the apostolic historic origins to the present ecclesial moment and ever onwards. According to such a distribution, the mysterious work of the sacrament is a relational communication or exchange rather than an objective or visible "thing" requiring interpretation or commentary, and ensures the unity between the two times, overcoming the division of anteriority and futurity, by beckoning towards a journey to be taken "beyond" all present points of reference.[37]

The publication of de Lubac's epoch-making study of eucharistic ecclesiology, *Corpus Mysticum*,[38] was attended by anxiety in more conservative theological circles, and at Rome, that

---

[35] *After Writing*, pp. 139–40.
[36] Ibid., p. 157.
[37] Ibid., p. 159.
[38] H. de Lubac, S.J., *Corpus Mysticum: L'Eucharistie et l'Eglise au moyen âge* (Paris 1948).

he was entering a plea for a more doctrinally undifferentiated perception of the Church-Eucharist relation at the expense of dogmatic teaching on the (incomparably) "Real Presence" in the Holy Gifts. That is also what Catherine Pickstock's introduction of the theme would lead one to suspect – until at the very close of *After Writing* one is struck by a breath-taking twisting of the tail (on which more anon). It remains strange that the *tour de force* of interpretation by which Pickstock will construe the historic Western liturgy as philosophy's consummation does not take as its material the late antique and Carolingian liturgies of the time of de Lubac's sources, but the Tridentine codification of the worshiping life of the immediately pre-Reformation Church, that Church where, she fears, reification of the eucharistic species and expropriation of the Liturgy by a clerical caste had reduced the power of the rites to shape Christendom's sacred city.[39]

This puzzlement should not be allowed to suppress the wonderment, the admiration, in both the Latin and the English senses of that word, which should be ours in following Pickstock's commentary on the historic Mass as yielding up, when approached aright, a distinctively Christian sense of reality – touching such dimensions as desire and hope, time and futurity, subjecthood and relation with others – all in their proper ordering to that plenary and unspeakable divine being before whom we can but stutter praise. And in Pickstock's study of the *Ordinarium Missae*, this feat is accomplished in a way that both recreates in Christian guise the Socratic-Platonic vision and indicates a resolution for the problems raised by the philosophical centuries ever since unfolding. As Dr. Gerald Loughlin has summarized the content of Pickstock's commentary on what others would call the "jumble" or "confusion" of the unreformed rite:

> The old Roman Rite maintains a syntactical complexity rich enough to express the involutions of Christian doctrine, and position the worshipping subject as one who is constituted in

---

[39] Though citing E. Duffy, *The Stripping of the Altars: Traditional Religion in England, 1400–1580* (New Haven and London 1992), she does not do full justice to its case for the lay appropriation of the late mediaeval liturgy.

and through such worship, who receives him or herself through the offer of praise. Pickstock traces, in immense detail, the stammering nature of doxology, whereby, through repeated invocation and petition, the worshipping subject requests the power of request, of approach and arrival, in order to find him or herself already arrived, already the donation of the divine, receiving him or herself through doxological dispossession, the sacrifice of prayer and thanksgiving. In this way, the liturgy imagines and constitutes an utterly temporal subjectivity, which is always arriving through divine donation, a non-identical repetition of the ceaseless donation that is the life of the Trinity, and which opposes the self-positing, static and spatial subjectivity of sophistic modernity, the subject of writing.[40]

And Pope Pius XII, alarmed by Henri de Lubac (the later cardinal), would be rejoiced by Catherine Pickstock the schismatical (alas!) divine. Whereas in Derrida's postmodernism, signs lose their efficacy, their validity, through that process of endless deferral described by Charlene Spretnak, the Eucharist understood in terms of transubstantiation restores what that covert nihilism had lost. That in which the Saviour's humanity is embodied, and which because it is the humanity of the Word incarnate that is flesh there has the divine Logos for its ultimate subject, is one reality with broken bread. *Pace* the Real Presence, this is indeed reality, and so not a sign if we are to think of signs as *counterposed* to the real. And yet, in Pickstock's words, it

> becomes a sign in being given to us, given as a promise or sign of future givings, and so given as the turning of all things into gift, which means also into sign, since a gift is a gift only in its signifying promise of renewed gift to come.[41]

And here we realize that it is not a Christianized retrieval of the ancient Greek wisdom at its best that Catherine

---

[40] G. Loughlin, "Rains for a Famished Land," in *Times Literary Supplement*, 10 April 1998, p. 13. At the Cambridge *Communio* Circle meeting where this paper was read, Pickstock stressed, however, that for her doxology makes possible a *fused* mode of written and spoken rhetoric – so at this point the contrast of the two should not be overdrawn.
[41] *After Writing*, p. 263.

Pickstock has attempted, but the placing of its intuitions on a wholly new basis constituted by the Incarnation and its continuation in the sacramental life of the Church. As she concludes, in the donation of self to which Christians are called by this sign that gives all signs their meaning, the body is not, as in Plato, left finally behind, but sacrificed together with the spirit in order that

> the spirit and the body together might be received back again on the eschatological morning.[42]

That linkage of anthropology to eschatology via the mystery of the Eucharist, joins Catherine Pickstock to such modern Catholic and Orthodox theologians as Louis Bouyer and John Zizioulas, while her plea for a defamiliarizing liturgy – not merely as distinct from, but as opposed to, a consciously modernizing one – relates her to sophisticated supporters of more complex and subtle rites than those currently found in the West, as for example the Bristol sociologist Kieran Flanagan.[43] But her most central plea is for the rebirth of a Christian ontology not, as hitherto, from the doctrines of creation, Christology, and the Trinity, but from the *reprise* of these and more as found specifically (by her methods!) in the doxological stratagems and formulae of the medieval Church. This is an approach which, I think, can only have been stumbled on by occasional and philosophically unreflective accident in the past. It constitutes, so it seems, a genuine novelty in the life of theology – and one that, unlike most innovations, really can claim to be "radically orthodox."

---

[42] Ibid., p. 273.

[43] K. Flanagan, *Sociology and the Liturgy: Re-presentations of the Holy* (London 1991).

INDEX OF NAMES

210